BASICS *of* AMERICAN POLITICS

A Short Guide to U.S. Political System and
Foreign Relations Current Events and Case Studies

MAY SAFA SALHA

An investment in knowledge pays the best interest.

—Benjamin Franklin

TABLE OF CONTENTS

PROLOGUE

As a lifetime student of politics and more specifically world affairs, I took it for granted that my passion for the complex geopolitical relationships existing in the world today was shared by all. I was wrong.

I remind myself that not everyone is obsessed with history and current events. People have other areas of knowledge and expertise. They excel in their own fields. But I can't help noticing the gaps. In my head, I am constantly correcting flaws.

Just the other night, I met this accomplished doctor at a charity fundraiser. When he asked me where I'm from—yes, I get asked that question ten times a day. I can't seem to get rid of the accent—I said I am an American citizen of Lebanese descent. He asked me where exactly Lebanon was. It's north of Israel. I answered more of his questions. No, we don't have deserts and camels. Sure there was war, but it's been over for decades. I was slightly surprised by the simple lack of information coming from such a highly educated man.

I get asked regularly by my friends to clarify the Arab-Israeli conflict because it's so complicated and hard to follow for them. Who do we root for? Can I explain it in simple terms please? And I do, and they listen. How about Islam, always in the news? What's the difference between Sunnis and Shiites? Which one is ISIS? Which one is Iran? Who are the terrorists from America's point of view? How about Pakistan? Is it in the Middle East? Are Pakistanis Arabs? And so on.

These are daily occurrences for me. Americans who forgot their history lessons or who are not current on present-day news. I also get asked a lot about American politics. Mostly by my Canadian or French or Lebanese friends. Why didn't Hillary Clinton win the presidency? Didn't she get more votes? Why do you allow guns in your country? What's the difference between a Democrat and a Republican? I find myself often explaining American politics in very simple terms. The way a teacher would explain it in a middle-school classroom.

A few months ago a bulb lit in my head. Most people don't know much regarding current affairs and not for lack of intelligence or education but simply for lack of knowledge on this particular subject. We live in times where nonfiction reading is less and less popular. Who has time to read scholastic books regularly? We want instant gratification, like getting our news online, even though we know it's not always factual. The result is a big mush of information attacking our brain.

So I decided to find a remedy. A kind of compromise. I decided to write a short handbook, more like a manual, where I talk about a variety of current events, each one of them discussed in a very short and straight-to-the-point section, all revolving around America and its relationships with other countries of the world. Each section is written like a straightforward uncomplicated lesson. Simple, short and factual.

Every section is totally independent from the others, where the reader can decide to learn about one topic and not choose to read all the others. What's the compromise again? It's not a long detailed book, yet it's more comprehensive and factual than online information in general. This manual is designed to be read quickly for the purpose of gaining factual knowledge about our internal politics and external relations without the pressure of research. That's my compromise.

So I wrote it, as you can guess, fairly fast. I pretended I was answering those questions I get asked most days. I made my kids read it. Then I asked my husband and my close friends to read it, and they all found it easy to understand and enlightening. I avoided personal opinions (which I'm known for) and stuck to facts. Yet I wanted to engage the reader. So I decided to end every section with some food for thought, with a few pros and cons to bring the topic to a close and to make the reader think about what was discussed.

If I have to describe this book in one sentence, I would say, it's a short simplified review of America and its geopolitical relationships—for those who would like to understand certain subjects without the inconvenience of going through a long complicated study.

Knowledge is power. Information is liberating. Education is the premise of progress, in every society, in every family.

—Kofi Annan

INTRODUCTION

This work focuses on the United States of America and its strategic relationships with other nations in different parts of the world.

It is natural to begin our quest for knowledge with the internal workings of government and the *founding principles* set forth in the *Declaration of Independence* and the *United States Constitution*. The United States has a unique responsibility for upholding and advancing those principles not only towards its citizens but all over the world. In the words of Thomas Paine "The cause of America is in a great measure the cause of all mankind". We can not fully grasp our position in the world today and our relationships around the globe if we do not have a solid understanding of our internal structures. In this context, the first three sections will be devoted to the U.S. Constitution, the U.S. government and the electoral process.

From the beginning, the purpose of U.S. foreign policy has been to defend the American constitutional system and push forward the interests of the American people. The next eight sections will therefore focus on the United States' external relations and geopolitical interactions in different parts of the world. I have carefully selected the regions that are relevant to current events and affecting U.S. policy today. This is not to imply that other areas of the world have less importance; I have simply attempted to narrow the scope of a study that is already far-reaching. In this context, I started with our neighbours, then moved towards our most impactful allies. I also focused on our main competitors on the global stage, our open enemies, and of course, on the international conflicts that have impacted the second half of the twentieth century till the present-day. Each nation or region of the world is briefly introduced for the purpose of clarity in a short historical overview, then examined in relation to U.S. foreign policy.

At the end of every section I added some *food for thought* in order to challenge our thinking process and debate our newly-acquired knowledge.

The last section naturally focuses on America's position in the world and the new challenges it faces in today's changing domestic and global dynamics.

Finally, it is important to note that the United States has always had a unique understanding of governing because its foreign policy is accountable to the American people. The basic premise has always been the implementation of liberty and justice *within* but also for others around the world. Hopefully, this short book will shed the light on those values of our Constitution and their effect on international relations today.

We have the oldest written constitution still in force in the world, and it starts out with three words, 'We, the people.'

—Ruth Bader Ginsburg

I.
THE U.S. CONSTITUTION

I will start our political enlightenment process with the Constitution of the United States. Simply because it is the *supreme law of the land*. If we do not understand the basic principles written in the Constitution, we will not grasp who we are as Americans. Obviously, for the purpose of this book, I will not go into Constitutional law or any deep analysis of the Constitution's meaning. What is important for us here is to understand the essentials relevant to our rights and duties as citizens. No more, no less. Let's keep it brief and simple.

The Founding Fathers of the United States created the U.S. Constitution as a follow up to and fulfillment of the Declaration Of Independence of 1776. It established America's national government, determined its fundamental laws and guaranteed certain basic rights for its citizens. It was signed on September 17, 1787 by delegates to the Constitutional Convention in Philadelphia. The goals were:

1. to form a more perfect union
2. to establish justice
3. to insure domestic tranquility
4. to provide for the common defense
5. to promote the general welfare
6. to secure the blessings of liberty to ourselves and our posterity

The Constitution originally comprised seven articles establishing the basic principles of our government. We have a government *of the people, by the people* and *for the people.* We are a *representative democracy,* which means, we vote for our representatives to make the laws on our behalf. Being a representative democracy is not unique to the United States, it is indeed the case in most modern liberal democracies today. Otherwise we would be a *direct democracy,* such as Switzerland, and we would get up every morning and legislate.

The Constitution lists our basic rights as citizens and protects us. *We The People.* That says it all. We are the ones who set up the government and decide our own fate. The government works for us and protects our rights. It exists to serve the citizens of the United States. The Constitution is the official recognition of individual rights, rules of law and separation of powers.

Granted, what works in theory is sometimes hard to see in praxis. We find greed and corruption in all walks of life. This is acknowledged here, but it is not the purpose of this work. I am discussing the Constitution and its original intent, which has not been disputed.

The Constitution lists three rights considered *inalienable.* In other words, natural rights that no government can take away from us. They are the rights to life, liberty and the pursuit of happiness. They are the very basis of America's independence. *We The People* give the power to government, and *We The People* can take it back. People are *created equal* is also a basic premise in the U.S. Constitution. Those ideas were originally coined in the Declaration of Independence which announced our independence from Great Britain and declared the American people *free* of British rule. The Founding Fathers believed that Great Britain did not respect the basic rights of people in the colonies.

There are two main types of government: nationwide and statewide. It's the idea of Federalism. The federal government is the national government. In their infinite wisdom, the Founding Fathers wanted to limit the power of the federal government. They feared abuses of power, like under the European monarchies, and wanted to prevent it from happening all over again in the United States. So they separated the powers into three federal branches: executive, legislative and judicial. I will go into that in more detail in the next section entitled U.S. Government.

It is important to note that the Founding Fathers believed that a government exists only if the people think it should. People create their own government and *"consent"* or *agree* to follow laws their government makes. This idea is called "consent of the governed" which is the basis of representative democracy.

The Constitution also has amendments, which are changes or additions. The Founding Fathers knew that laws can change as the country grows. They did not make it easy to modify the Constitution for fear of it losing its meaning. A special convention had to be requested by two-thirds of the states or the Congress of the United States would have to pass it by a two-third vote in the Senate as well as the House of Representatives.

The Constitution has 27 amendments; the first ten are called the Bill of Rights, which establish the most important rights and liberties of all Americans. They were added in 1791 and passed by Congress.

What are those rights? Let's stick to the essentials. I will keep it short.

1. Freedom of expression (speech, religion, assembly, press and to petition the government)
2. The right to bear arms
3. No soldiers shall quarter in any house during peacetime
4. Freedom from search without a warrant
5. The right to not testify against yourself and freedom from being tried twice for the same crime
6. The right to a speedy and public trial
7. Right to an impartial jury trial of civil cases
8. Freedom from cruel and unusual punishments
9. Rights retained by the people
10. Powers reserved to the states

For more than 200 years, the United States has aimed to become a "more perfect union". Our country is independent because of the determination of the Founding Fathers who established great ideals and principles guided by equality and fairness. The reasons colonists came to America are still valid today. They came seeking personal and religious freedom, political liberty, economic opportunity but also escaping persecution.

The U.S. Constitution is certainly one of the most influential legal documents ever to be written, if not the most influential in existence. Many countries around the world have used it as a model and a framework for their own constitutions. It is a living document, constantly interpreted by the Supreme Court in order to adapt it to a changing world. In many ways, it has remained *unchanged* and *unchallenged* since its creation. Courts may quarrel over its *interpretation*, but they never question the wisdom of its underlying principles. The document was written over two hundred years ago but still plays an integral role in our daily lives.

Learning about our Constitution help us understand our rights and responsibilities and allows us to fully participate in the American political process.

Food for Thought

In the news today we often hear contradictory arguments about the meaning and limitations of certain rights. Most controversial is the Second Amendment, pertaining to our right to bear arms. Is there a limit to the types of weapons? And did the Founding Fathers foresee the risks of modernization and the lethal effects of certain weapons and their negative impact on society and security?

What is clear is the right to own a weapon that allows us to defend ourselves and our property. There's no question about the clarity of this right. What is questionable remains the infringement of that right on the rights of others to enjoy security and peace. It depends on the way we interpret the Second Amendment.

How about some individuals asking to limit the freedom of the press? Does the press have infinite liberties? Do we have the absolute right to say anything we want at any time we want? Or are there limitations to that right?

Now we better understand the fundamental purpose of our Constitution: to protect the basic rights of all Americans. The U.S. Constitution also has another essential job: to set up and to define the government. This leads us to our next section.

Power must never be trusted without a check.

—John Adams

II.
U.S. GOVERNMENT

In this section I will explain government in a simple and straightforward way. I will thereby discuss the basic elements that we all need to know in order to understand how things work in American government. Again I will refer to the Constitution of the United States, since it is the law of the land. As discussed in the previous section, the Constitution protects our rights as Americans. It also sets up the government and defines the role of the government.

The United States government is, first of all, a democracy. This means that the people rule. As we discussed in the previous section, it is also a representative democracy, where people elect leaders to represent their viewpoints.

It is also a republic. This means that the head of state (the president) is elected by the people—unlike a monarchy, for example, where the throne is inherited through a family dynasty or an authoritarian regime, where a strongman assumes power through nondemocratic means.

The United States government is also a constitutional democracy, operating under a set of laws and principles outlined in the Constitution.

Finally it is a federal system of government, where the national government shares responsibility with the state governments and the municipal governments.

We are "a government of laws and not of men." In other words, everyone must obey the law, including citizens, leaders and government.

No one is above the *rule of law*. The government protects all people *equally*. Yes, I acknowledge that there are people who will subvert the law by various means. That is not to be covered in this writing. I am dealing with the highest intent proposed by the U.S. Constitution. In constitutional democracies, people are willing to obey the laws because the laws are made by the people through their elected representatives. It is important to understand that when all people are governed by the *same* laws, the individual rights and liberties of each person are better protected. In other words, the rule of law makes sure that government protects all people equally and does not violate the rights of any.

What is our system of government? In Articles I, II and III, the Constitution establishes three branches of government.

First, the *legislative branch*. Congress (comprising both the Senate and the House of Representatives) makes the federal laws, which in turn apply to all the states and all the people.

Second, the *executive branch*. Its job is to enforce the laws that Congress passes. The president is the head of the executive branch. His vice president and cabinet are also part of the executive branch.

Third, the *judicial branch* or the Supreme Court, which is the highest judicial power. It has one major and crucial job: to make sure that the federal government follows the Constitution. The Supreme Court interprets the Constitution on a daily basis.

This system is also called *separation of powers* and *checks and balances*. In simple terms it means the government's power is divided into those three branches to assure no one branch becomes too powerful. They restrain and block each other in order to limit power and to ensure the rights of the people are not violated. Each branch will *check* or *balance* the other. For example, the Senate (legislative branch) can block or threaten to block a treaty signed by the president (executive branch). In this case, the legislative branch is "checking" the executive. Or the U.S. Supreme Court (judicial branch) can reject a certain law passed by Congress. In this case the judicial branch is "checking" the legislative branch. I view it as a beautiful synchronization, where things work together yet challenge each other. The Founding Fathers vehemently opposed concentrating too much power in any particular body of the federal government in order to avoid any form of tyranny.

What else do we need to know about the U.S. government?

The president is both the head of state and the head of government. He is also the commander in chief of the military. He has the power to sign treaties with other countries —or to withdraw from treaties for that matter—though Congress must ratify any treaties with foreign nations. The president chooses his ambassadors to represent the United States around the world and to carry out the nation's foreign policy.

The president can also set national policies and propose laws to Congress. He can name the top leaders of the federal departments, print money, raise armies and declare war. Most important, he appoints the judges of the Supreme Court to fill any vacancy. The Senate can reject the president's choice if deemed unacceptable. This is another perfect example of checks and balances.

The same applies to the Cabinet members. They should be confirmed by the Senate. The role of the Senate is to oversee the executive appointments and to deem them acceptable. Examples of cabinet positions are the secretaries of various departments: agriculture, attorney general, commerce, defense, education, energy, health and human services, homeland security, housing and urban development, interior, labor, state, transportation, treasury, and veteran affairs (fifteen total). Their job is to advise the president.

The president, as well as the vice president, are elected for a term of four years. If the president dies or is incapacitated, the vice president takes over, and the next in line is the Speaker of the House of Representatives.

The Congress passes laws. How does that work? Either the House or the Senate can propose what is called a *bill* to address an issue. Each house votes separately for the bill. If it passes both houses by a majority vote, it's sent to the president. If the president signs the bill, it becomes federal law. He can also veto the bill. In this case it will be sent back to Congress and requires two-thirds vote in both houses to pass. This is another great example of checks and balances intended by the Constitution to prevent any one branch from gaining too much power. Congress comprises two chambers, the Senate and the House of Representatives. One hundred senators represent our fifty states. All states have equal power in the Senate, since each state has two senators. They are elected for six-year terms.

On the other hand, the House of Representatives, while based on population, has been capped at 435 members, due to the passage of the Permanent Apportionment Act of 1929. The number of representatives varies from state to state, depending on the population of each state. The term for representatives is two years. Also six non voting delegates represent the District of Columbia as well as other U.S. territories such as Puerto Rico, Guam, Northern Mariana Islands, U.S. Virgin Islands and American Samoa.

How about the Judiciary? Its job is to review the laws, to resolve disputes and, most important, to decide if a law is constitutional. In other words, the Supreme Court makes sure every law is consistent with the Constitution. That's why we are called a *constitutional democracy*. The Supreme Court makes the final decision pertaining to cases that have to do with federal laws and treaties. It also rules on disagreements between states. It is limited in power over states, yet it can decide if a state action or law conflicts with the U.S. Constitution or federal law.

There are nine justices on the Supreme Court—eight judges and one chief justice. They are appointed for life. There are also lower federal courts and judges.

We discussed the powers of the federal government. How about the states? They have certain powers too, including schooling and education, police and fire departments, driver's licenses and marriage requirements, taxing people, legalizing marijuana, land zoning, traffic regulations etc.. States cannot declare war or print money. Each state has its own capital city, a governor, a legislature and state courts. Although each state has its own constitution, they can not conflict with the U.S. Constitution. The federal and state governments also share some powers, such as the ability to tax people.

Finally I will briefly discuss our economic system.

We are a *capitalist economy*, where most businesses (of all sizes) are *privately owned*. Our economy is motivated by profit and competition. The market determines prices. It's a *market-driven economy* where producers and consumers are free to interact for goods and services. In other words, the American economy is that of a free market; meaning, there's substantial freedom to buy, to sell and to produce in a competitive environment.

It is also called a *mixed economy*. Although it is regarded as a capitalist regime, the U.S. government is in control of major aspects of the economy, such as health and education. It also imposes regulations on certain sectors of the economy to ensure equitable gains for all its citizens. This makes it a mixed economy, a shift from pure capitalism. Therefore, privately owned businesses as well as government *both* play necessary roles.

It is important to note that the emphasis on private ownership arises, in part, from American strong beliefs about personal freedom. From the early days of the Founding Fathers, Americans have feared excessive government intrusion, and they have sought to limit government's authority over individuals, including its role in the economic sphere. In addition, most Americans believe that an economy characterized by private ownership is likely to operate more effectively than one with considerable government ownership. There are limits to free enterprise, though. Americans fully understand that some services are better performed by public rather than private enterprise.

Despite some reservations about where to draw the line between the general belief in free enterprise and the need for government management in certain sectors, the mixed economy existing today has been remarkably successful.

We covered some of the basic notions of government in this section. I tried to summarize hereinabove what I deemed most important to understand how our U.S. government works.

Food for Thought

Every day the concept of checks and balances is challenged in political life. Does the system of checks and balances complicate the policy-making process and make it more time-consuming? Does it actually work in restraining the influence of a demagogue? Or as James Madison said, does it prevent abuse of power by having the government limit its own influence? How about when one party gets control of multiple branches of the government or both houses of Congress, does this weaken the *separation of powers* intended by the Founding Fathers? Allowing one set of interests to prevail at the expense of the public interest? A few pros and cons to enhance our thinking process.

Today, we witness the interaction between the president and Congress, the role of the Supreme Court trying to resolve issues crucial to citizens. We may see discussions, arguments, even open hostilities, but, at the end of the day, the system works exactly the way it was set up to do: always striving to limit powers and to avoid autocracies. The beauty of the synchronization of all three branches transcends the current events and strengthens the institutions.

We the people are the rightful masters of both Congress and the courts, not to overthrow the Constitution but to overthrow the men who pervert the Constitution.

—Abraham Lincoln

III.
U.S. POLITICAL PARTIES
AND ELECTIONS

This section discusses the electoral process. Let's simplify the concepts and keep it related to modern politics, since the purpose of this book is not to discuss U.S. history but to understand how the political parties operate today and how the elections work. The U.S. Constitution did not establish political parties. Nothing in our Constitution expresses or implies the need for political parties. It was a concept the Founding Fathers preferred to avoid. In other words, political parties are an extra-Constitutional invention, devised by politicians to push forward their agenda and enhance the interests of the people they represent.

Let's start with the obvious. What's a political party? It's a group of people who share the same views, opinions and values about policies, power and government. They organize into a party and promote candidates who reflect their beliefs and who eventually run for office with the hope to implement those common values. The purpose is to gain power and to shape public policy.

The two major political parties in the United States today are the Republican and Democratic parties. Our system is a two-party system, as opposed to the multiparty systems in European democracies, for example, where several political parties compete for power or contrary to the one-party system of authoritarian regimes, where one party snatches power and imposes its rule on the country.

While recently some alternative parties have become more popular here in the U.S., the Democratic and Republican parties remain the two largest parties, holding the majority of the seats in the Senate as well as the House of Representatives. The two main parties have opposing views on several key issues in the economic, military, political and social spheres.

What is the main difference between the Democrats and the Republicans? The main difference lies indeed in their political orientation. The Democratic Party is *left leaning*, liberal and mostly associated with progressiveness and equality. The Republican Party on the other hand is *right leaning*, traditional and associated with economic freedom, equity and the concept of survival of the fittest.

Given those differences, the two political parties have clashed on a number of issues, such as taxes, gun laws, voter ID laws, abortion, same-sex marriages, immigration, the death penalty, health care, individual rights versus collective rights and the limits on the size of government.

To summarize, Republicans believe in strong border controls, the death penalty, tax cuts for the rich and the use of firearms. They are against same-sex marriages and abortion, while supporting private health-care systems and believing in a limited role for government.

The Democrats support more open immigration policies and more regulations in the use of firearms. They believe that the rich should pay more taxes than the lower classes and that the government should have a bigger role in socio-economic matters, including health care. They oppose the death penalty. They are in favor of same-sex marriage and free choice for women.

However, it is important to note that the two parties aren't always fundamentally opposed. America's Democratic and Republican parties are so large and diverse that the line gets blurred and sometimes difficult to identify. Unlike in France, for example, where the parties are ideologically antagonistic, ranging from Communist to extreme right on the ideological spectrum. In fact, we can find extremists and moderates on both sides of the parties here in the United States. But the majority of individuals lie somewhere in the middle. The changing dynamics of domestic and international issues often lead people to change views on important matters.

In other words, while the traditional positions of the Democratic and Republican parties are quite different, the reality is rather muddled, and their views do not oppose as clearly.

The responsibility of the American citizen is to participate in the democratic process by voting. Even though voting is not mandatory, it is crucial for citizens to choose leaders who will represent them as well as their interests and values. The only way a democracy can properly function is through the participation of more and more of its citizens in the voting process.

Citizens can vote on the state and federal level. They vote for their representatives in Congress as well as for the president of the United States or for the governor of their state. They also vote locally. At the age of eighteen anyone can vote as long as they are citizens (and as long as they meet other requirements as necessary, per laws of individual states). Citizens play an active part in their communities; the only way a democracy stays strong and dynamic is when Americans actively engage in the political process, not just by voting but also by volunteering, running for local board positions, organizing, polling, and engaging with their senators and representatives about issues that are important to them.

The president is the only official elected by the entire country. The Founding Fathers thought that European kings had too much power, so the Founding Fathers limited the power of the president of the United States by having the people elect a president every four years. Before 1951, a president could serve as many terms as he liked. There was no limit. After the Twenty-Second Amendment to the Constitution, the president is now limited to two terms (four years each) for a total of eight years.

Unlike other democracies, where each person has one vote, and, therefore, the candidate with most votes wins the election, the United States has a different (and slightly peculiar) system.

We elect our president through the Electoral College, per the Twelfth Amendment to the U.S. Constitution. It's a bit complicated, but I'll simplify it as much as possible. Each state has a certain number of electors—the number of senators and representatives combined. For example, the state of New York has two Senators (like all states) and twenty-seven

Representatives (based on population) in Congress. Therefore, it has twenty-nine electors in the Electoral College. Wisconsin has two Senators and eight Representatives in Congress; therefore, it has ten electors in the Electoral College. So it's all proportionate, based on how dense the population for each state. It's an indirect election of the president by electors (amending the original function of the Electoral College as set forth in Article II of the Constitution). The Electoral College simply means all the electors of each state added together.

Each state counts its own ballots, certifies the number of votes cast by its representative electors and sends it to Washington, DC, to determine which candidate got the most votes and, therefore, is elected president. A candidate must receive an absolute majority of electoral votes (currently 270) to win the presidency and the vice presidency. If no candidate wins that majority, the House of Representatives chooses one of the top three presidential electoral vote winners, while the Senate chooses one of the top two vice presidential electoral vote winners.

It is important to note that the electoral college is somehow unique to the American electoral system and viewed by many as controversial in nature. The Founding Fathers originally designed the electoral college as an indirect boundary against a national majority overpowering individual states. In other words, the Founding Fathers believed that the various states will lose too much of their power toward the federal government. So they created a new system based on a direct popular election *within* each of the states. They wanted an extra layer of electors as part of the system of checks and balances to prevent a radical "mobocracy" (or tyranny of the masses) and consequently to restrain too much power in the hands of the President or what they feared to become and "imperial presidency". As James Madison stated "the great danger is that the majority may not sufficiently respect the rights of the minority". Therefore the Founding Fathers created a system where the people have less power by denying them the right to directly elect a president as is the case in most modern democracies and by transferring more power in the hands of those state "electors".

There are several criticism to this system of elections mostly pertaining to the fact that it is simply less democratic than a *direct vote* by the people. In a deeply polarized electorate such as in the U.S. today, the loser of the national popular vote can win the Electoral College vote and become president even though more people voted for the "loser" candidate or winner of the popular vote. This seems to defy democratic principles. Also this system gives more power to the smaller and less populated states when in most modern democracies results are concentrated more in urban centers. Additionally, presidential elections (as we have witnessed in 2000 and 2016) come down to a handful of swing states (such as Pennsylvania, New Hampshire, Ohio, Iowa, Florida, North Carolina, Colorado and Nevada) and not necessarily reflect the national will. Many argue that the Electoral College is an "antiquated" system that was created to keep the people out of the government. Fear of the mob or the "tyrannical majority" does not exist in modern times as people got more educated and advanced in their civic notions. In other words, this same criticism advocates that people should be allowed to directly elect the president and should not be forced to accept the will of the electors. The majority should effectively rule.

Changing the system would require an amendment to the Constitution, since it is the only way to change a stipulation of the document itself. There are pros and cons to this theory. Some believe that changing the electoral college system will destabilize our system of government as it will certainly be a fundamental alteration of what has worked for a long time. However, others believe that the change would be for the better in the sense that it will make the United States a stronger and more modern democracy.

Food for Thought

The biggest objection to the Electoral College system is that it has (especially in the recent 2000 and 2016 presidential elections) denied victory to the winner of the popular vote. One may question the wisdom of the Founding Fathers and accuse them of being slightly undemocratic. Why can't the people elect directly? Why the middleman (or elector)? Surely one can question the process. The Founding Fathers did not trust the ordinary people to directly elect the president. They also did not take into consideration the eventual existence of our two-party system in political life. Certainly some food for thought.

At the end of the day, the Electoral College was a compromise between the president being elected indirectly by the people (democratic) and the president being chosen by Congress (not very democratic). The compromise worked for years to come. Citizens vote for electors who eventually choose the president.

A people... who are possessed of the spirit of commerce, who see and who will pursue their advantages may achieve almost anything.

—George Washington

IV.
OUR NEIGHBORS:
CANADA AND MEXICO

After discussing in the previous three sections the workings of our internal government, we can now turn to our external relations. The most natural place to begin is with our neighbors.

The United States is the world's third-largest country in size with an area of 3.797 million square mile (9.8 million square kilometer) and a population of 325.7 million as of 2017. Located in North America, it is bordered to the east by the Atlantic Ocean and to the west by the Pacific Ocean. Along our northern border is Canada, and our southern border is Mexico. We are extremely lucky in our geography, since we have the luxury of nonaggressive friendly neighbors to our north and south with the two oceans to the east and west. Our very unique geographic position has given us a huge degree of security and the capacity to focus on our own business as well as international affairs, without the stress of the constant inconvenient presence of a predatory neighbor.

Canada

Let's look north toward Canada. The United States and Canada have one of the world's most exceptional relationships. They occupy the majority of North America while sharing the "world's longest undefended border."

Both sovereign nations, they rely on each other for trade, security and afflu-ence. Despite a history of war (which we will not get into here, since mod-ern times are the focus of our study) and a cultural distrust (Canada insists on its own unique cultural identity being separate from the American cul-ture in general), the two countries stand as an example of interdependence, alliance and cooperation that is a model to the rest of the world.

I will not go into historical details of what brought us to this excel-lent modern-day relationship with our northern neighbor. Instead I will focus on what we need to know in order to understand current events. The United States and Canada share common democratic values and ideals such as equality, respect for different cultures, safety, peace, liberty, human rights and much more. The similarities and common interests are present in everyday life. Canada is also heavily influenced by American popular culture such as music, Hollywood movies, TV shows etc.., to the point that Canadian cultural products are funded and protected by the government in order to preserve their identity. There are some differences, though. Unlike the United States, Canada rejects the notion of extreme individu-alism. Canadians prefer the idea of community, society and common sup-port reflected in their widespread social services, health care and equality among provinces.

U.S. defense arrangements with Canada are more extensive than any other country. The Permanent Joint Board on Defense, established in 1940, provides policy-level consultation on bilateral defense matters as both countries share mutual security commitments. Bilateral law enforcement cooperation and coordination have always been excellent and have become even better after the September 11 terrorist attacks. Canadian and U.S. fed-eral and local law enforcement personnel fight cross-border crime on a daily basis which have resulted in highly secure crossings.

Canada is also a member of NATO, the G8 (Group of 8) and G20 (Group of 20). Both countries work closely on international issues such as law enforcement, environmental protection, free trade, fighting terrorism and more.

Historically, trade has been an area of contention (if not open dis-agreement) between the United States and Canada. After prolonged negotiations over trade disputes that have plagued both countries, an agreement was reached in 1987, which eventually became known as the North American Free Trade Agreement (NAFTA) in 1994 after extended to Mexico too. NAFTA fundamentally reshaped North American economic relations, promoting unprecedented integration between Canada's and the United States' developed economies and Mexico's developing one.

When this agreement finally came into effect, the American-Canadian economic relations were fundamentally changed. It's true that the agreement did not end all the disputes, but it had a lasting effect of dramatically growing trade between the two countries with the U.S. taking 80% of Canada's exports, and Canada receiving 70% of its imports from the United States. The implementation of NAFTA gradually removed tariffs on countless products (particularly related to agriculture, textiles and automobiles) exchanged between the two nations. Canadian companies operating in the United States employ more than 500,000 Americans. Therefore, we can safely say that the trading relationship between the U.S. and Canada helps both countries in growing stronger respective economies, encouraging economic growth, eliminating barriers, creating jobs on both sides of the border and competing globally.

Politically the two countries are friends and allies. This does not mean that they get along on all issues or that both countries don't have ups and downs regarding some of these issues. It is not always easy for Canada to have such a powerful neighbor who expects Canada to join in all the U.S. foreign affair endeavors, militarily and diplomatically. There is certainly a sense of frustration with American foreign policy emanating from how Canadians view America's role in the world compared to how Americans perceive those same global activities. The pressure can take its toll. Canada has always struggled to impose its own sense of nationalism and distinction in a world mostly dominated by U.S. policies and influence. Not wanting to be "American" is one of the defining points of Canadian national identity.

This being said, it is extremely difficult to imagine a future where the fundamentals of our American-Canadian relationship aren't stable and friendly. Canada's foreign and defense policies are usually in harmony with the United States' policies. Areas of contention do exist (for example, the Vietnam War, the response after 9/11 or, more recently, climate-change disagreements and tariff disputes), but they are relatively few. Friends can disagree. But the two sovereign nations have been a great example of living peacefully and trading continuously with each other. This economic integration, as well as long-term democratic traditions on both sides, make cooperation a matter of fact.

Today, with the new policies of the Trump administration -mostly pertaining to nationalism as well as trade and tariffs- there seems to be a shift in mood. The political developments in the United States have created unease about the state of relations on both sides of the American-Canadian border. President Trump is perceived to have an expansionist economic policy combined with protectionist measures (higher tariffs) which could negatively impact Canada.

On environmental issues, President Trump's policies are widely viewed as reactionary by Canadians and, in turn, having an irreversible impact on the environment. Also the fate of NAFTA, given Trump's apparent protectionism and "anti-Mexican" sentiments, is of great concern to Canada, particularly when it comes to the president's suspicion of all trade agreements. On the surface, it is the exact opposite of Prime Minister Justin Trudeau's inclinations. Negotiators from Canada and the United States were finally able to reach an agreement (October 2018) on a new free trade pact that will include Mexico. The United States-Mexico-Canada Agreement (USMCA) updates and replaces NAFTA which President Trump had labeled a "disaster" and vowed to cancel.

As serious as those issues seem to be in the minds of both Americans and Canadians, it is unlikely that long-term damage will result in their bilateral relations. The history of intercooperation and peaceful friendship will most likely transcend the setbacks of shifting policies.

Mexico

How about Mexico, our southern neighbor? The United States and Mexico share a two-thousand-mile-long border. The relations between both countries are strong and vital yet are complicated by issues that do not exist with our northern neighbor, mostly due to economic disparity and immigration.

No other country in the world directly impacts America's homeland security more than Mexico. Security cooperation between both countries is, therefore, indispensable. Today, both countries have a highly extensive and sophisticated bilateral law enforcement relationship, sharing information related to migration, border security, criminal threats, human smuggling and narcotics on both sides of the border. Despite the rhetorics of the Trump administration and any so-called "anti-Mexican" sentiments, the relationship seems to be working as well as ever because it is in the best interests of both countries to maintain such relations.

Unlike the situation with Canada, the scope of the U.S.–Mexican relations is much broader. It impacts the lives and the livelihoods of millions of Americans as well as Mexicans. It pertains to trade, commerce, citizen security, education, migration, drug control, entrepreneurship and much more. In addition, hundreds of thousands of legal border crossings occur each day—and both ways. One and a half million American citizens live in Mexico, and Mexico is the number one foreign destination for U.S. travelers.

NAFTA paved the way for a closer U.S.–Mexico relationship on security, trade and the fight against narcotics. When negotiations for NAFTA began in 1991, the goal for all three nations was the integration of the developing economy of Mexico with the highly-developed economies of the United States and Canada. Over the years, NAFTA has had positive effects on the Mexican economy increasing growth, encouraging foreign investments, boosting exports of Mexican products and most importantly providing more middle class jobs that enabled more Mexicans to lift themselves from poverty. The purpose was also to discourage illegal immigration from Mexico to the United States. Economists largely agree that NAFTA has provided considerable benefits to the North American economies. Regional trade increased sharply from roughly $290 billion in 1993 to $1.1 trillion in 2016. Today, Mexico is a strong promoter of free trade, maintaining free trade agreements with the most countries of any nation in the world.

The issue of illegal immigration has for a long time plagued both countries. Mexicans attempt to illegally cross the border every day. Various U.S. administrations have attempted to curtail those activities by implementing tougher immigration laws. Even though the number of illegal immigrants has stabilized in recent years (after a period of rapid growth), Mexico remains the leading country of origin for most unauthorized immigrants to the United States. Many Americans believe that Mexican immigrants are a drain on the American economy taking jobs away from the lower-income American workers and imposing significant costs on the U.S. government. However others believe that the migrants benefit the economy by working for low wages.

Another growing problem between both nations is the alarming volume of drug trafficking that has taken place in recent years. Drugs continue to pour into the United States despite the efforts of the DEA (Drug Enforcement Administration), the border patrols and other enforcement agencies. Illegal drug abuse has risen to an epidemic-level, not only affecting lives but imposing huge costs on the U.S. government.

Despite those serious issues of contention (illegal immigration and narcotics), Mexico and the U.S. share high levels of cooperation to counteract those activities. It is in the interest of both the United States and Mexico (and Canada) to continue strengthening their economic cooperation and integration. After all, Mexico is the third-largest U.S. trade partner (after China and Canada), and enormous investments exist on both sides.

Of course important variables are still at play that could affect U.S.–Mexico relations in the near future, such as the fate of NAFTA negotiations and the construction of a border wall. As mentioned in the above section pertaining to Canada, there was finally a new trade agreement reached between all three North American neighbors, the USMCA, which at least for the time being has ended the tensions pertaining to trade relations. The border wall issue remains a point of contention between both countries as no solution has been reached.

Today, the relationship between the United States and Mexico remains strong and has certainly proved durable despite bumps in the road. Both sovereign nations have significant interests in maintaining positive and productive relations. Neighbors who share a nearly two-thousand-mile-long border and trade $1.5 billion in goods and services should eventually find a way to make things work.

Food for Thought

Is it in the best interest of the United States to renegotiate NAFTA or to end it? Would it achieve positive results for the American economy or create new problems, such as more impoverished Mexicans attempting to illegally cross our borders? How about the USMCA? Will the new trade deal achieve favorable results or will it intensify the rising political, economic and cultural mistrust among all three nations? Should we maintain those close all-encompassing historic ties with our North American neighbors, or should we shake the boat and weaken cooperation with these bordering countries?

It is not tolerable, it is not possible, that from so much death, so much sacrifice and ruin, so much heroism, a greater and better humanity shall not emerge.

—Charles de Gaulle

V.
OUR NATO ALLIES:
GREAT BRITAIN, FRANCE
AND GERMANY

Now let's look at our allies overseas. We will start with our main Western allies in Europe. The focus will be on Great Britain, France and Germany. None carry the weight as much as these three, considering our history with them as well as their economic, diplomatic and military influence around the world. We will look at a bit of history in this section in order to grasp the full implication of our special alliances. I will keep it as brief as possible, not to digress from our main focus, which is on current affairs, and not to create a long historical thesis.

Until the advent of what is popularly known as *Brexit* in Britain in 2016, all three countries noted above were part of the European Union, which, as a whole, shared an excellent relationship with the United States. The European Union and the United States enjoy close ties and are the two most closely linked economic regions in the world.

During the Cold War, western European nations offered solidarity to the United States in exchange for security and a role in the partnership that reshaped the world post WWII. This arrangement gave them a "sense of power" without the global responsibility that comes with it. European security depended on the United States because American and European interests were perceived to be the same. The transatlantic partnership was successful and peace was maintained decades after the end of the Cold War.

The United States and the EU also have the world's largest investment relationship, based on a commitment to open, transparent and nondiscriminatory international investment policies. This reciprocal relationship embodies a number of shared core values, such as a high level of competitiveness, strong protection for investors, neutral settlement of dispute and solid national security considerations. These mutual interests provide the basis for transatlantic cooperation and for regular consultations between these two allies at the government level in all matters. In brief, the United States and the EU share a historical relationship which is strengthened by cooperation on military defense, trade and shared values.

Great Britain

Let's start with Great Britain. The United States gained independence from Britain in 1776. In this context, we can consider it our *"motherland"*. The relationship has had its ups and downs, including wars. Yet, after World War I, it seems to have stabilized and eventually grew into what would become one of the most successful military alliances in history. World War II only strengthened the relationship as both the U.S. and Great Britain emerged victorious from the conflict against Nazi Germany and its allies reestablishing the preponderance of democratic values as fascism was defeated.

The United States has no closer ally than Great Britain, and British foreign policy emphasizes close coordination with the United States, reflecting the common language and shared democratic practices of the two nations. After WWII, relations were further strengthened by their alliance in the Korean conflict, the Persian Gulf War, Operation Iraqi Freedom and in Afghanistan. The U.S. and Great Britain were central to the Cold War policy of *containment* of communism. Britain's role as a founding member of NATO laid a basis of military cooperation between the two nations where they both continually consult on foreign policy issues and objectives. They also intensely cooperate on national security and regularly share intelligence.

Today both sides like to define Anglo-American relations as a *"special relationship."* The concept was originally conceived by British Prime Minister Winston Churchill following WWII. The history of the "special relationship" has, to a large degree, been defined by personalities, various security issues and Europe. It has not always been easy. The establishment of NATO in 1949 led to a deepening of military ties, but the alliance was not exempt of challenges.

For example, the United States and Great Britain highly disagreed over Britain's handling of the 1956 Suez Crisis with Egypt. In another instance, Britain was angered by the U.S. invasion of Grenada, a British Commonwealth nation in 1983. As Britain's imperial power was fading in the second half the twentieth century, the importance of collaborating with the United States in international affairs became more urgent.

Personalities played a huge role. Just like Winston Churchill and FDR shared a closeness and a common understanding of the world, so did Margaret Thatcher and Ronald Reagan, Tony Blair and George W. Bush, David Cameron and Barack Obama. The relationship between Theresa May and Donald Trump seems to have hit a few bumps but has not reached a serious level of unfriendliness.

Some of these paired-off personalities shared an ideological vision and a personal friendship, others a more pragmatic look at cooperation but always within a context of entente and shared objectives. When Great Britain left the European Union in 2016, in what was popularly called "Brexit," the move was not perceived as a threat to the status quo by the United States but as an internal matter.

It is interesting to note that British ideas, classical and modern, have exerted a profound influence on U.S. economic policy, most notably the writings of historian Adam Smith on *free trade*. Also, cultural exchanges in the areas of art, music, theatre, royalty, fashion and much more continue to blossom. There is a history of mutual admiration and cultural curiosity between the United States and Great Britain that transcend political, military and economic considerations.

We will revisit Great Britain at the end of this section when we discuss NATO.

Food for Thought

There are still many undecided factors with regard to the final destination of the negotiations between Great Britain and the European Union. Can Brexit become a future challenge to U.S.-British relations? As of now we have not witnessed a dramatic change in the nature of the relationship. But the actual exit from the European Union is not scheduled till March 2019. Will the U.S. greatly miss the influence and global perspective that Great Britain brings to EU decision-making? As our closest ally? Could the move negatively impact the "special relationship"? Or will the present state of affairs prevail?

France

How about France? What are the cornerstones of the relationship between the United States and France?

We are traditional allies with essential political and military cooperation. Despite some significant differences, our political philosophies are the same. Though both countries may critically compete in economic and trade situations, they have never been at war with each other, which cannot be said about our other European allies, such as Britain or Germany.

France played a role in America's Revolutionary War against England as the United States' first ally in providing military support, and the U.S. played a crucial role during WWII, ensuring France's very survival against German occupation. The French gave us the Statue of Liberty to underline and emphasize our common ideological and political values.

Furthermore, both the United States and France are democratic and liberal in their core values. Our differences remain tactical and never strategic. When it was a matter of survival, the U.S. and France always stood together against authoritarianism, even when their leaders were not necessarily close on a personal level. We may share core values ideologically, yet the details aren't always cohesive. The French are very attached to the notion of "the *common good*" and *equality* (based on Jean-Jacques Rousseau's political philosophy, which influenced Enlightenment throughout Europe in the 1700s and beyond), while we Americans are extremely unforgiving to anything that can affect our "inalienable rights" of *liberty* and *individual freedom*.

Franco-American military, political and intelligence cooperation remains essential. The two nations work closely on many issues, most notably in fighting terrorism, limiting the proliferation of weapons of mass destruction and dealing with regional problems, including Africa, the Middle East and Central Asia. As one of the leading powers of the European Union, France worked to prevent Iran from developing nuclear weapons. France is also a major contributor, along with the United States, in defeating ISIS, as well as a leader in the peace process pertaining to the Arab-Israeli conflict.

France and the U.S. are fierce rivals and competitors in trade, finance and industries. France is very particular on being totally independent from the United States' domineering foreign policies. France considers itself a major international player in its own right, with strong influences emanating from its unique position as an old imperial power with present-day *Francophone* authority all over the world. After WWII, France wanted to re-assert its international identity as a nation capable of holding its own against superpowers such as the Soviet Union and the United States. France feared to be perceived as a weakened power and failing old empire. The only way France was to be respected again as a strong nation and leader in world affairs was through maintaining a strong French identity free of foreign influence and pressure. This attitude is directly related to the psychological trauma of defeat in the face of Nazi occupation. After WWII, efforts were made to focus on a strong and self-sufficient economy in turn allowing France to maintain its independence vis a vis the United States and other emerging powers.

France's position as a cultural power (francophonie) with widespread influence all over the globe allows it to act as moderator and arbitrator in world conflicts and crises. This unique cultural position as well as past glory (*La Grande Nation*) also allow it to be fiercely independent from its allies' policies and impose its own voice on international matters.

France's approach toward the United States is as a "friend and ally but not aligned." In other words France will always have its own foreign policy agenda, which often generates tensions between the two nations. For example today, Donald Trump and Emmanuel Macron are at odds on several foreign policy issues, such as the Iran nuclear deal, global climate change and trade. Despite those specific points of conflict, France maintains a pragmatic approach to the transatlantic partnership. It perceives the Trump administration's "disruptive" policies as both a challenge and an opportunity to push forward Europe as a credible power at the global level.

Food for Thought

Today, both the United States and France strive to preserve continuity and stability in Franco-American bilateral relations despite certain disagreements and international rivalry.

What do we understand from our relationship with France? Friends and allies? Sure. But we share an extremely independent and not always supportive relationship regarding each other's policies.

Germany

Let's look at Germany, our present-day ally with a history of enmity. Germany was our enemy in WWI and WWII. In both wars, the American involvement had a definitive effect in the defeat of the German Empire and Nazi Germany. The defeat of Nazi Germany was the highest priority and a matter of survival for the continent of Europe. Eventually, the United States played a major role in the occupation and reconstruction of Germany after the defeat of Adolf Hitler.

Unlike France and Britain, Germany historically did not share ideological values with the United States. In fact, until 1945, both nations have been on the opposite side of the spectrum. The United States emphasized democratic values, whereas Germany—since its inception as a unified state in the late 1800s—has been ruled by either authoritarian monarchs or the totalitarian expansionist Nazi regime during the 1930s and 1940s that was responsible for widespread war, the occupation and destruction of most of Europe, and the horrific genocides of millions of Jews and other ethnicities. In 1945, at the end of WWII, Germany was divided into East Germany and West Germany until its reunification in 1990.

During the second half of the twentieth century until the present day, the United States became one of Germany's closest allies and partners outside the European Union -West Germany at first then unified Germany-. The United States understands that the security and prosperity of both nations significantly depend on each other. There has been disagreement on some key policies; the U.S. expects Germany to play a more active role in stabilizing the globe that is proportionate to its powerful economic weight. Also the United States wants Germany to play a more active military role worldwide, but the Germans strongly disagree. They have an innate reluctance to become a military power. Foreign involvements are tightly restricted by German law and parliament, with the Germans being extremely "sensitive" about their warlike past.

There are also other areas of contention. For instance, there is the matter of trade and economic interest. Germany's economic ascent in Europe has a lot to do with its ability to export German products, because it produces much more than it consumes. In order to sell its surplus, Germany need markets such as the EU and the United States. The Trump administration is critical of the growing German surplus, which in turn could lead to a potential trade war under the new U.S. protectionist trends. Finding a common ground on those critical policy issues is going to be a tough task.

Despite those disagreements, Germany remains one of the United States' closest allies in Europe; they are trading partners, sharing vital political, economic and security interests as well as common institutions.

In the political and economic sphere, Germany stands at the center of European affairs. It plays a key role as a member of NATO, the G7 (Group of Seven) and the G20 (Group of Twenty). These three organizations host international summits where leaders from the world's advanced and emerging economies meet to discuss critical global issues. Germany's leadership position and influence in Europe are key to promoting democracy, human rights and economic development all over the world.

There's coordination between the United States and Germany at the highest levels. In the last few years, both nations have worked closely together to counter Russian aggression in the Ukraine, to negotiate a political solution in Syria and to implement the Iranian nuclear deal.

On the world stage, Germany seems to have found a new confidence under the leadership of Angela Merkel. Germany is an economic giant with influences all over the globe. This has led to a certain level of rivalry with the United States, despite the convergence of other shared interests.

Recently the relationship has been strained due to the clash of personalities between Chancellor Angela Merkel and President Donald Trump. The U.S. president is particularly insistent on Germany shouldering more of the defense burden within NATO. Europe's defense dependency on the United States serves as a reality check. A new trend seems to be developing, where Germans believe that Europe, with Germany as its central subject, must be "*weaned*" from the American protection that has existed since 1945. It is the reflection of the public mood and the ""anti-Trump" sentiments.

This is not the official policy though, and U.S.–German cooperation is still very much alive.

Food for Thought

Will Germany and the United States drift further apart due to some serious disagreements on political, military and economic matters, or would the hard-earned cooperation of the post-unification era be maintained? Will this create a widespread anti-American sentiment in Germany? Will the U.S. tolerate the emerging German confidence and assertiveness? Just a few questions to help us think beyond the norm.

NATO

We finally get to NATO. The fact is, focusing on economic prosperity worked well as long as the European countries could rely on their security from their NATO alliance and their military protection from the United States. This has been a point of contention between Europe and the Trump administration, with President Trump wanting the European nations to contribute more to their own defense.

What is NATO? The North Atlantic Treaty Organization is a military alliance between three nuclear powers (the United States, Great Britain and France) and twenty-six other North American and European countries, signed April 4, 1949. Historically it was the first peacetime military alliance entered by the United States, operating as a system of collective defense whereby each member-state agrees to mutual defense against an external attack.

At its inception, it was a defense mechanism against the possibility of attack from the Communist Soviet Union. Its original purpose was to unify and strengthen the Western allies in response to a potential aggression from the Soviet Union and its Warsaw Pact allies. After the dismantlement of the Soviet Union, NATO's role changed, and its fundamental duty became to safeguard the freedom and security of its members, by political and military means, and a more and more important role in crisis management and peacekeeping.

It is important to note that NATO promotes democratic values and is committed to the peaceful resolution of disputes. If diplomatic efforts fail, NATO has the military capability to undertake what is called *crisis management operations.*

Food for Thought

Today, with Russia led by an increasingly belligerent Vladimir Putin, Turkey under a newly authoritarian Tayyip Erdogan, the Middle East more violent than ever, Britain preparing to leave the EU and apparently a more isolationist America, the very purpose of NATO is being questioned, pushing Europe to take a more active and forefront role in its own defense. The questions remain: How relevant will NATO be in the future? Will it maintain the crucial unifying and protective role it has played since the end of WWII, or will it become, as President Trump says, "obsolete"?

Mr. Gorbachev, tear down this wall!

—Ronald Reagan

VI.
RUSSIA

The relationship between the United States and Russia is highly complex. It ranges from solid alliance to open enmity. It is among the most critical bilateral relationships in the world, with implications well beyond the two nations themselves. For more than two decades, the relationship has cycled between periods of cooperation and confrontation. While recent tensions over Ukraine and Syria are now restraining the relationship, the United States and Russia continue to need one another to achieve international priorities. We will look very briefly at Russia's modern history in order to comprehend today's state of affairs between the two countries.

In 1917, Russia witnessed the Bolshevik Revolution (or the Russian Revolution), which dethroned the tsar and installed a Communist regime. In the same year, the United States entered WWI, and Russia exited. They both fought on the same side, for the Allies, yet not together. In the early years following the revolution, Russia was plagued by political upheaval and civil war. Relations between the new Soviet Union and the United States were fluctuating and uncertain. The American government feared the revolution could be exported world-wide and affect the U.S. domestically, especially during the *Great Depression*. The communist ideology was perceived as a threat to the American capitalist system and the American way of life. In 1933, the United States officially recognized the Soviet Union. The move brought a degree of stability to the bilateral relations. However, from an ideological perspective the two nations stood on the opposite sides of the spectrum; the Soviet Union was an authoritarian communist regime with widespread human rights abuses against its own citizens, while the United States valued democracy and individual freedom.

During WWII (1939–1945), as the devastating spread of fascism threatened the very existence of European democracies, once again we find the United States and the Soviet Union fighting on the same side in their efforts to defeat Nazi Germany and its allies. Working to end fascism initially strengthened U.S.–Soviet relations. However, with postwar power consolidation and the rise of the Communist ideology, things would not remain stable for long.

Tensions mounted as both the United States and the Soviet Union actively pursued power and influence across the globe. Both nations were capable of producing nuclear weapons, which in turn prompted an arms race, known as the Cold War. Both countries became global superpowers.

Despite the tensions and numerous escalations (for example the Bay of Pigs crisis in 1961 or the Cuban Missile Crisis in 1962 both under President John F. Kennedy), the two powers did not directly engage in military aggression or war with each other, though the United States was actively engaged during the 1950s throughout the 1980s to stop the spread of communism all over the world (Korea, Vietnam, South America, Cuba, etc.). Both the United States and the Soviet Union competed in nuclear armaments and the development of space programs. It was a race for global domination.

Containment was the official U.S. foreign policy toward the Soviet Union and its Warsaw Pact allies during the Cold War years. It is a geopolitical strategy stating that communism should be contained and isolated or it would spread to neighboring countries in what is called the *domino effect*. The Cold War instigated a strong wave of anti-communism within the United States, not just from a foreign policy perspective, but also on the popular and cultural levels where the hatred of anything "communist" or associated with communism was predominant.

In 1991, the Soviet Union collapsed. It dissolved from within and became Russia again, officially ending the Cold War. At the beginning of that new era, the relationship between Russia and the United States was generally cordial. Both sides made efforts to limit the proliferation of nuclear weapons. At this point Russia, a struggling young democracy, was considerably weakened. It had lost extensive territory when several former Soviet Republics (such as Georgia, Ukraine, Armenia, Belarus, Azerbaijan, Estonia, Lithuania, Latvia and many more) separated from the new Russia and formed their own independent nations. Russia was also plagued by economic and social issues; even its military was considered outdated and obsolete by modern-day norms. It lost its superpower status.

At the end of the 1990s, relations between the two old rivals started to cool off again with the military operations against Serbia and Montenegro, two republics composing Yugoslavia at that time. The disagreements between the United States and Russia became more serious when Vladimir Putin assumed power in Russia in the early 2000s. His style of leadership was -and still is- characterized by a renewed Russian assertiveness in international affairs. Putin did not view Russia as a secondary power but as a leader on the international scene with a say in regional conflicts and diplomacy.

The United States and Russia experienced tensions concerning Georgia, Ukraine, Poland, Iraq post–9/11, Iran, Syria and more. Putin used every tactic in an effort to regain Russia's superpower status. From manipulating trade policies, to encouraging divisions within NATO, to expanding his sphere of influence on Russia's neighbors and the Middle East, he bluntly pushed ahead his agenda of a strong Russia.

The ongoing civil war in Syria -which began in 2011- showcased Russia's role as an international player, with Putin supporting the regime of Bashar al-Assad. The U.S. and Russia could not agree on the critical situation in Syria as well as Russia's role. A tentative agreement was reached in 2013 with the Obama administration whereby Syria's chemical weapons will be placed under international control and eventually destroyed. However, the Syrian Civil War continues to this day (2018) with no diplomatic solution in sight.

Tensions between the United States and Russia reached a peak when in 2013, Edward Snowden, a U.S. government contractor, stole and released hundreds of thousands of secret U.S. government documents, then fled to Russia and was granted political asylum. He was wanted by the U.S. prosecutors for theft and espionage. This situation further aggravated relations between the two countries. Snowden remains in Russia as of September 2018.

Other sources of tensions between the United States and Russia pertain to the crisis in Ukraine in 2014, which escalated into the annexation of Crimea. The Obama administration (as well as the EU and other allies) did not retaliate militarily against the Russian aggression but instead imposed punitive sanctions, targeting Russia's major energy, financial and defense companies. The crippling sanctions angered Russia, viewed as interference in its internal affairs and its direct spheres of influence, which, in turn, harmed the bilateral ties. Relations were at their worst since the Cold War.

When one would think things couldn't get worse between the United States and Russia, the U.S. accused Russia of meddling in its presidential election campaign of 2016. The accusations were serious. Russia was blamed for being behind massive cyber-hackings that aimed at influencing the election and discrediting the entire U.S. political system and its democracy. Donald Trump was widely seen as the pro-Russia candidate, with alleged connections between his campaign and Russian interests. Russia, as well as President Trump, deny those allegations.

Unfortunately, despite a positive personal connection between President Putin and President Trump, the bilateral relationship between the two countries has not improved. In 2017, the United States imposed a new round of sanctions on Russia pertaining to Iran, North Korea and Syria. The war of words escalated. Eventually diplomats were expelled on both sides in connection with the election-meddling accusation—described by top U.S. intelligence officials as an "internal attack on our democracy".

Despite the escalating tensions, a ray of hope for Russian-American cooperation still exists. Recently, President Putin presented President Trump a series of proposals related to nuclear arms control, as well as other measures to reduce the risks of military clashes between the United States and Russia especially in areas such as Syria where both nations have military presence.

To characterize our relationship with Russia as complex is an understatement. We are not open enemies, but we are not friends. We have serious points of contentions and hostilities, yet we are not against certain forms of cooperation. There's fierce competition on the world stage, yet both presidents seem to have a warm personal bond. While acknowledging there were still challenges ahead in improving bilateral relations, both presidents seem satisfied at the outcome of their 2018 summit.

Food for Thought

Will the relationship between the U.S. and Russia deteriorate more as our points of contention increase? Will it reach a problematic level, where we can be open enemies on the international stage due to Russia's newfound assertiveness? In other words, a return to Cold War mentality? Or will the personal affinity between both presidents lead to a new era of cooperation and rapprochement?

No matter what's happening in the Middle East...the emotional, critical issue is always the Israeli-Palestinian one.

—King Abdullah II of Jordan

VII.
THE ARAB–ISRAELI CONFLICT

This section covers one of the most complicated and controversial conflicts in history. The debate is still ongoing as to "who's right, and who's wrong," with both parties clinging passionately to their own views. This topic will always create a disagreement. It is difficult to have a perfectly objective description of the relevant events, as each side views them from diametrically opposite perspectives. The truth barely exists; facts are analyzed according to one's own "feelings and emotions", and historical objectivity remains foggy.

Our purpose here is to understand the role of the United States pertaining to Israel, Palestine and, most important, the *peace process.*

I will explain the events from a factual position. Simplifying a highly complicated situation won't be easy, but, for the sake of clarity, I will do my best to stick to a simple timeline. A bit of history is a must.

The Arab-Israeli conflict is all about the land. It's a ruthless struggle for the heart and soul of a small piece of land called Israel by some and Palestine by others. Let's go back to when it all began.

For centuries there was no such conflict. The land of Palestine was inhabited by a multicultural population, mostly Muslim (about 86%) some Christian (approximately 10%) and very few Jewish (no more than 4%). They lived peacefully among each other. In the late 1800s, a European group of extremist Jews, known as Zionists, decided to settle in Palestine and create a Jewish homeland. They immigrated from Europe to Palestine, which created alarm among the indigenous population. In 1917, the British government issued the Balfour Declaration, which supported the establishment of a Jewish state in Palestine. The declaration gave legitimacy to the Zionist movement.

After WWI, the League of Nations granted Britain a mandate to rule over Palestine (in other words, Palestine became a British colony). With the rise of Nazi Germany and the persecution of the Jews in Europe, Jewish immigration to Palestine increased tremendously. The Arab population objected, and eventually fighting broke out between both sides, culminating in a full-fledged revolt against the British presence.

The Arabs, in what became known as "The Great Revolt" rose against the British mandate, demanding Arab independence in Palestine and the end of any Jewish immigration with the purpose of establishing a Jewish state.

The British government attempted to negotiate a deal. The Peel Commission Report of 1937 suggested the creation of a small Jewish state and a much larger Arab one. The Jews accepted, but the Arabs rejected the compromise. The situation turned into full-scale civil war by 1947, which peaked into the first Arab-Israeli War in 1948 when five Arab countries (Egypt, Jordan, Lebanon, Syria and Palestine) joined the Palestinian side in the aftermath of Israel announcing its independence.

At this point the United States offered a de facto recognition of the Israeli provisional government. During the conflict, the U.S. maintained an arms embargo against all belligerents, not taking sides with any of the fighting parties to preserve its neutrality.

In 1947, the United Nations adopted what is called the Partition Resolution (United Nations Resolution 181) that would divide the former British mandate into Jewish and Arab states. Jerusalem would remain under international control, administered by the UN. The Palestinians refused to recognize the resolution. The United States remained neutral, though it did support the UN resolution. It also sought a compromise by encouraging further negotiations between Arabs and Jews in the Middle East.

At the end of the 1948 war, Israel gained some territory formerly granted to the Palestinians, while Egypt and Jordan retained control over the Gaza Strip and the West Bank respectively. When the Zionist forces defeated Palestinian militias and the Arab armies, more than seven hundred thousand Palestinians had fled or had been expelled from their homes. Some ended up in refugee camps in the Gaza Strip and the West Bank. Others began lengthy exiles and were never allowed back. The Israeli military adopted a free-fire policy, allowing soldiers to shoot returning refugees. Today more than seven million Palestinian expats and refugees are found around the world.

The United States was not involved with the armistice negotiations. Its main fear was that the instability in the Middle East would interfere in the international balance of power with the Soviet Union.

An uneasy peace was maintained for about eighteen years until 1967. At this point, Egypt became deeply involved in the Arab-Israeli conflict. It amassed troops on Israel's borders. The tension escalated as the nationalistic government of Gamal Abdel Nasser used strong war rhetorics on a daily basis. Israel, fearing for its safety and survival, launched a preemptive strike, known as the Six-Day War. Israel captured all of the Sinai from Egypt, all of the West Bank from Jordan, the Golan Heights from Syria and the Old City of Jerusalem. It was a devastating blow to the Arab side.

Five months later, the United Nations Security Council passed Resolution 242, calling for the withdrawal of Israeli forces from the territories it had occupied during the 1967 strike. At this point, Israel had already allowed the establishment of civilian settlements in the West Bank, which was against international law. Today, more than 40% of the land in the West Bank falls under the settlers' control. It is still one of the most difficult points of contention between the two opposing sides.

In 1973, Egypt and Syria (under Presidents Anwar Sadat and Hafez al-Assad) attacked Israel, which sustained initial heavy losses. Eventually Israel defeated both armies. The attack became known as the Yom Kippur War. The defeat led to the Camp David Accords in 1978, brokered by the United States. Egypt and Israel signed the peace agreement, formally ending the state of conflict—if not outright war—that had existed between the two countries for the last thirty years.

Under the terms of the Camp David Accords, Israel returned the entire Sinai Peninsula to Egypt, and, in return, Egypt recognized Israel's right to exist. The two countries subsequently established normal diplomatic relations. The agreement is still in effect today. The United States played a crucial role under the Carter administration in brokering the peace treaty.

In 1982, Israel invaded neighboring Lebanon in order to remove the PLO (Palestinian Liberation Organization) fighters operating from southern Lebanon after repeated attacks on Israeli settlements in the north. Israel occupied West Beirut and expelled the PLO from Lebanese soil. Israel hoped to sign a peace treaty with Lebanon which did not occur. Outrage followed Israel's role (alongside Lebanese Christian militia allies) in the Sabra and Shatila massacres of Palestinians and Lebanese which led to Israel's gradual withdrawal to the south of Lebanon and the establishment of what became known as the South Lebanon Security Belt. The United Nations condemned the massacre and declared it to be a an act of genocide and a violation of international law. A year later, two suicide bombers killed 241 American and 58 French multinational peacekeepers in Beirut. The incident marked the largest single-day loss for the U.S. military since the Vietnam War. The 22-year Israeli occupation of southern Lebanon came to an end in the year 2000 after Israeli troops suffered continuous attacks on the hands of the Lebanese Shiite military group Hezbollah.

Hostilities continued on the Palestinian front. In December 1987, rioting broke out among Palestinians living in the Israeli-occupied territories of the Gaza Strip and the West Bank as well as in Jerusalem. It soon became a widespread popular rebellion, known as the *First Intifada,* directed at the continued Israeli occupation of the West Bank and the Gaza Strip.

In 1993, an agreement (the Oslo Accord) was reached between the PLO (Palestinian Liberation Organization) and Israel under the supervision of the United States. It resulted in the majority of the Gaza Strip and the major Arab cities in the West Bank coming under Palestinian control—in other words, a form of self-governing for the Palestinians.

This agreement did not end the conflict. Violence kept erupting, and the Palestinians resorted to repeated suicide bombings in public places. The wave of violence was supported and funded by Hamas, a more extreme Palestinian opposition group that refused to recognize the previous agreement between the Palestinians and Israel, as well as the existence of Israel. They regularly fired rockets into Israel, resulting in three short wars in 2008, 2012 and 2014.

Israel was forced to send ground troops into Gaza and eventually withdrew and built an effective missile defense system against the Hamas-Palestinian rockets. It also held Gaza under a blockade to control its borders and to limit who could get in and out. Since 2014 an uneasy state of semi-quiet existence prevailed.

Why is this conflict so painful and difficult to resolve? Let's try to understand the positions of both sides. Life for the 1.5 million Palestinians who live in the Gaza Strip is difficult. Israel controls the coastline and all the entry and exit crossings into Israel. There is no working airport. Because access is so restricted, few goods make their way into Gaza, which often results in shortages of food, such as fresh meat and vegetables, making everyday life strenuous. There are often power cuts. Large numbers of people are unemployed because businesses can't get their products in and out of Gaza. Therefore, the socio-economic situation is extremely unstable if not desperate. The blockade has ravaged the economy and severely reduced the jobs and goods available for the population. The blockade also isolates the population from the natural resources and amenities that people require to live and work.

On the other hand, Israel feels compelled to maintain this blockade situation for security reasons. The Palestinian (pro-Hamas) suicide bombings and rocket strikes made life terrifying for millions of Israelis who fear those continuous *terror* attacks on civilians. Israel -with the help of Egypt- has maintained this blockade for over a decade, which it says is necessary to prevent Hamas from smuggling in weapons and material used for digging tunnels into Israel. Hamas is regarded as a terror group by the West and is sworn to Israel's destruction. Hamas fired over 2,500 rockets and mortars at Israel, almost all directed at civilian targets such as border towns as well as larger cities, including Tel Aviv. Israel blames Hamas for the economic conditions in Gaza. It feels it has no choice but to maintain the blockade, because the group continues to concoct ways to attack Israel.

The United States, under several administrations, has worked hard to settle the fighting between the Palestinians and the Israelis. The purpose is to unite Gaza and the West Bank into one independent country, Palestine. Israel won't agree to this unless it feels safe and also until Hamas recognizes Israel's right to exist, which to this day, it hasn't. There are numerous sticking points, such as the fate of the Israelis who settled in the West Bank, the fate of the Palestinian refugees and, most important, the status of Jerusalem as the holy city of three religions—Judaism, Christianity and Islam.

The United States views Israel as a top ally. We have strong ties with what we perceive as the only country in the Middle East that shares our values. Throughout the decades, American support for Israel has been massive, including billions of dollars in aid (about $118 billion to date) and diplomatic backing (half of all American vetoes of UN Security Council rulings effectively blocked resolutions critical of Israel).

Originally the United States viewed Israel as a buffer against Soviet influence in the Middle East and supported Israel accordingly. The reasons behind this support include deep sympathy for Israel among the American public, the influence of the pro-Israel lobby and, as we said above, the American ideological affinity with the region's most stable democracy.

The United States was the first country to recognize Israel as a state in 1948. In addition to financial support (over $3 billion annually), the U.S. participates in joint military exercises, military research and weapons development with Israel. The United States is also Israel's largest single trading partner. The two nations have had a free trade agreement since 1985. The U.S. has long defined Israel's survival and security as important to its own national interests.

Despite this fundamentally close relationship, occasional tensions erupt between the United States and Israel. It was particularly obvious in the clash of personalities between President Barack Obama and Prime Minister Benjamin Netanyahu, mostly regarding the Iran nuclear deal and the increasing number of Israeli settlements in Palestine. The Trump administration has led to renewed warmth between the two governments, culminating in the decision to formally recognize Jerusalem as the capital of Israel in 2018, which infuriated the Palestinians who view Jerusalem as their own capital and holy city.

Food for Thought

Did the United States relinquish its position as primary mediator in the *peace process* by taking so unequivocally the side of Israel pertaining to Jerusalem? Would this position weaken the influence of the U.S. as a main actor in the Middle East? Despite a historic closeness to Israel, the United States has always managed to keep the door of diplomacy open with the Palestinians. Recognizing Jerusalem as Israel's capital angered Palestinians as well as Arabs, who now turn to other countries of influence in search for peace. Will this affect the United State's historic role as the dominant and reliable diplomatic power in world affairs particularly in the Middle East?

Even more serious is the reaction at home. The move reflected a growing partisan gap inside the United States, with Republicans and Democrats on opposite sides of the spectrum. There was unprecedented criticism of Israel. Is making Israel a partisan issue in the United States safe for the special bilateral relationship? Or will it create a rift and an actual threat to the very foundations of the U.S.–Israeli alliance?

Where is the justice of political power if it executes the murderer and jails the plunderer, and then itself marches upon neighboring lands, killing thousands and pillaging the very hills?

—Gibran Khalil Gibran

VIII.
SAUDI ARABIA AND IRAN

Why Saudi Arabia and Iran? Why are we devoting an entire section on those two countries?

For decades, U.S. policy in the Middle East has been shaped by its relationships with both Iran and Saudi Arabia. Today, next to Israel, they are the main powers in the region. Their rivalry, ideologies and military interventions have increased their influence dramatically throughout the Middle East and beyond.

Saudi Arabia and Iran have long been regional rivals. Two powerful neighbors, they are locked in a fierce struggle for regional dominance on both sides of the Persian Gulf. Tensions between the two recently escalated. We will look at each one of them separately, then try to understand their respective roles as far as U.S. policy is concerned.

Saudi Arabia

Saudi Arabia is a Sunni-dominated kingdom and home to the birthplace of Islam and its holiest sites (Mecca and Medina). It is also one of the wealthiest countries in the world as well as a top oil exporter. Ruled by an authoritarian monarch, it does not tolerate any form of dissent. The Sharia (or Islamic Law) is the law of the land. Today, King Salman, Crown Prince Mohammed bin Salman, and the royal Al Saud family hold power over every aspect of government and wealth. For example, until 2018, Saudi authorities have banned women from driving cars and denied them other rights. The Saudi government champions a very strict interpretation of the Sharia (based on the Wahhabi ideology) and funds religious schools around the world.

Providing security for the oil-rich Saudi Arabia as well as the rest of the Persian Gulf states (Bahrain, Iraq, Kuwait, Oman, Qatar, and the United Arab Emirates) has been a U.S. foreign policy priority since WWII. Saudi Arabia is the second leading source of imported oil for the United States, providing more than one million barrels per day of oil to the U.S. market. American companies were responsible for much of the oil produced in the region throughout the 1970s, and the Saudis have been an important U.S. partner throughout the Cold War. U.S.–Saudi military cooperation peaked during the First Gulf War in 1991 when the United States sent troops to free Kuwait after being invaded by Iraq. More than half a million U.S. troops stationed in Saudi Arabia and the neighboring Persian Gulf states, which in turn fueled anti-Western feelings and criticism of the Saudi royal family for allowing foreign troops on what is perceived as sacred Muslim soil.

A wave of popular anti-Saudi sentiment arose in the United States after the 9/11 terror attacks when fifteen of the nineteen hijackers were identified as Saudi citizens. Saudi Arabia was accused of fueling and financing the rise of jihadi terrorism around the world.

Saudi Arabia has a predominant leadership role in the Middle East based on its Sunni dominance and its capacity to use its wealth to spread financial aid and to affect policies. Saudi Arabia fears Shiite Iran wants to dominate the region. Therefore, Saudi Arabia is fundamentally opposed to Iran's growing influence as well as its political and military involvement all over the Middle East.

Since 2015, Crown Prince Mohammed bin Salman (with the support of his father King Salman) has waged a long destructive war in neighboring Yemen. The air campaign has targeted the Iran-backed Shiite rebels known as Houthis. Saudi Arabia has also backed anti-government Sunni rebels in Syria who are fighting to remove Syria's President Bashar al-Assad, a close and vital ally to Iran. The move appears to be a strategic shift in Saudi policy as Saudi Arabia is now openly challenging Iran's expanding influence in the region instead of doing it from behind the scenes as was the case in the past. There is an attempt to show the world as well as regional foes (most notably Iran) that Saudi Arabia is not just an economic but also a military power capable of imposing its will on neighboring countries. This newly assertive foreign policy is exacerbating the already existing instability in the region.

Additionally, the Saudi Crown Prince (also known as MBS) is setting out a wave of unprecedented internal reforms called "*Vision 2030*" with the purpose of modernizing Saudi Arabia and transforming its economy. The goal is to reduce Saudi Arabia's dependence on oil, diversify its economy, and push forward public services such as infrastructure, health, education, recreation and tourism. The reforms are minimal by western standards but certainly a step forward for traditional Saudi Arabia. The prince is also seeking to limit the overwhelming power of the ultra-strict religious clerics as he slowly moves the country toward a more modern path. Despite those efforts, the Saudi regime remains an absolute monarchy with no real concept of individual freedom or democratic values.

Regardless of its newly aggressive foreign policy, Saudi Arabia remains a key U.S. strategic ally. Despite this close alliance, various American administrations have voiced criticisms over human rights abuses, the export of the kingdom's austere interpretation of Islam, terrorism financing and the lack of democratic representation. With the help of the United States, Saudi Arabia has one of the best equipped militaries in the region and is among the biggest arms importers in the world. Common economic, security and strategic interests are likely to help maintain strong ties between the United States and Saudi Arabia for the near future, especially reflected in the Trump administration's renewed vows of friendship and cooperation.

Iran

On the other hand, Iran became an Islamic Republic in 1979, when the U.S.-backed Shah of Iran was overthrown by Shiite clerics and Ayatollah Khomeini assumed political power. As a modern theocracy (combined with elements of democracy in government structure), Iran challenges Saudi Arabia in its role as leader of the Muslim world. Today, Iran is the leading Shiite power in the region. Current Supreme Leader Ali Khamenei has the final say on major foreign and domestic policy issues. He also control the armed forces and the internal security apparatus. Just like Saudi Arabia, Iran has been and still is criticized for its human rights abuses. It may have a complex and unusual political system combining elements of modern Islamic theocracy with *democracy*, but it remains authoritarian in nature. Religious laws and religious courts interpret all aspects of life. The President of the Republic might be elected by the people but the ultimate power remains in the hands of the religious clerics and the Supreme leader. Contrary to popular belief though, modern Iranian society is not strictly religious, it is a clash between tradition and modernity, secularism and religion.

After the 2003 overthrow of Iraq's President Saddam Hussein and the diminishment of Iraq's regional position, Iran's regional influence grew considerably. Its influence is mostly witnessed in its support to President Assad of Syria in his fight against Sunni opposition groups and the so-called *Islamic State* (ISIS). Iran's elite Islamic Revolutionary Guards have been instrumental in defeating Sunni *jihadists* in Syria as well as in Iraq. Many of those jihadists are funded by Saudi Arabia in its attempt to strengthen Sunni groups in Syria and to limit Iranian control.

Saudi Arabia and Iran also clash in Lebanon. Iran believes Saudi Arabia is trying to destabilize post-war Lebanon, where the Iran-backed Shiite movement Hezbollah is part of the government. Saudi Arabia, on the other hand, fears the extreme influence of Iran in Lebanon, where it has allies and supporters. It is a very fragile balance of power.

Iran is reported to have one of the most advanced missile systems in the region. It is also a major oil exporter. Since the 1979 revolution when

Iran became an Islamic Republic, Iran has considered the United States as its main enemy -besides Israel- and regularly blames the United States for attempting to destabilize its regime.

In many ways the rivalry between Iran and Saudi Arabia can be compared to the Cold War between the United States and the Soviet Union. They do not directly engage each other in fighting but are involved in a variety of proxy wars around the region (Syria, Lebanon, Iraq, Yemen, etc.). They are actively attempting to contain each other's religious and military influence as well as competing for regional dominance.

For a long time, the United States has seen Iran as a destabilizing force in the region. A major cause of concern is the safety of the Persian Gulf. Saudi Arabia and Iran face each other across this maritime border. Fighting in the waters of the Persian Gulf would be catastrophic. The main fear will be an escalation into a much broader conflict. For the United States and other Western nations, freedom of navigation in the Persian Gulf is essential for international shipping and oil transportation.

Another significant cause of concern arises from Iran developing a nuclear program. The Obama administration worked hard to curtail this risk. No one wanted to see Iran become a nuclear power. In 2015, the five permanent members of the UN Security Council (The United States, Russia, Britain, China and France), plus Germany, agreed with Iran on a deal to prevent it from building a nuclear bomb. In exchange, certain international sanctions were lifted. Iran received billions of dollars of its own previously frozen funds and opened its market to foreign investors.

The Iran nuclear deal (Joint Comprehensive Plan of Action or JCPOA) took years to negotiate and was endorsed by the UN Security Council, reinforcing it as *international law*. It was also approved by the U.S. Congress. Inspectors from the UN nuclear watchdog, the International Atomic Energy Agency or IAEA, are in charge of monitoring Iran's compliance. Iran did comply, according to those IAEA reports. The deal was a success story of international and multilateral diplomacy. The Trump administration did not perceive it as such and exited the deal. With this decision, the administration discarded years of diplomatic work that had led to an extremely rigorous set of restrictions and inspections guaranteeing that Iran would not develop nuclear weapons. The door was also slammed on the possibility of a new era of *detente* between the United States and Iran. It remains to be seen whether exiting the deal and imposing strict sanctions might have future negative consequences for U.S. security in the region.

In 2018, the Trump administration signaled to Saudi Arabia that it would avoid criticizing its destabilizing actions in the Middle East. Instead, it blamed only Iran, the kingdom's regional rival, for funding terrorism and creating "havoc" in the area. The administration failed to acknowledge that Yemen's current conflict escalated dramatically in 2015, when Saudi Arabia intervened in the war. It is important to note that Iran *also* interfered in the conflicts in Yemen as well as in Syria and Iraq. In other words, both Saudi Arabia and Iran share responsibility in destabilizing the Middle East as they compete for regional power and influence.

The United States views Iran as an adversary and Saudi Arabia a friend. Yet Saudi Arabia's new activism is making the region extremely volatile. The Saudi leadership views Iran as an existential threat and seems willing to take extreme action to confront Iran's rising influence.

Food for Thought

So many questions arise from those complicated relationships. Can the United States keep supporting its old ally Saudi Arabia despite its newfound belligerence which can further destabilize the regional status quo? Or will the United States play a role in curtailing Saudi Arabia's behavior?

What about Iran? Will ending the nuclear deal drive Iran into more aggressive behavior? Or will it increase Iran's legitimacy because of its compliance, in turn isolating the United States internationally for ending the deal? Can the Trump administration lose credibility among its allies for breaking international law by exiting the deal? Or can the U.S. impose its will regardless of international resolutions? Most importantly, does withdrawing from the deal harm the United States' ability to negotiate future non-proliferation agreements with other nations, such as one with North

Korea? So many questions persist, yet as of now, it is difficult to predict the long-term implications of the volatile behavior in this part of the world.

Occasionally, the tree of liberty must be watered with the blood of patriots and tyrants.

—Thomas Jefferson

IX.
CRISIS IN THE LEVANT:
SYRIA AND IRAQ

This section will cover the ongoing wars in Syria and Iraq as well as the United States' role from the beginning of the crisis until today. I will not cover the historical events that led to the current state of affairs; instead I will briefly look at some of the triggers that lead to this crisis, a crisis that has affected the entire world, whether it's related to the expansion of terrorism or to the humanitarian refugee disaster.

Iraq

It all started in Iraq. In 2003, the United States invaded Iraq and deposed Iraqi dictator Saddam Hussein. Saddam Hussein formally rose to power in 1979 as part of secular sunni minority elite -the Baathists- that ruled Iraq. He suppressed several movements, mostly Shiites and Kurdish, and was widely condemned for the brutality of his dictatorship. In 2003, a coalition led by the United States invaded Iraq to depose Saddam Hussein after he was suspected of possessing weapons of mass destruction. He was later on convicted by an Iraqi court for crimes against humanity and sentenced to death.

The roots of ISIS (the Islamic State in Syria and Iraq) trace back to 2004, when the militant organization, first known as Al Qaeda, formed in

Iraq. Its purpose was to remove Western occupation and to replace it with a Sunni-Islamist regime.

The United States and the West were perceived to be the enemy, occupying a land that wasn't theirs. The movement was a direct reaction to the U.S. decision to invade Iraq. The main objective behind the invasion and subsequent occupation of Iraq was to free Iraqis from tyranny and implement a western-type democracy. Another strategic objective for the United States was to protect one of the world's largest oil reserves. It is safe to say that the U.S. did not succeed in implementing those goals. Instead of bringing democracy to a struggling nation, the ill-implemented policy backfired into a full-blown civil war between the Iraqi Shiite majority and the Sunni minority who supported Saddam Hussein during his rule.

When the United States decided to dismantle the Iraqi civil and military services, thousands of Sunnis formerly loyal to Saddam Hussein were left without jobs and an identity. Al Qaeda chose to capitalize on their anger and waged an insurgency against U.S. troops in Iraq. Even though Saddam Hussein was *Baathist* and secular, his ex-intelligence and military supporters found a common cause and identified with the Islamist jihadis of Al Qaeda. They quickly radicalized. They also waged a sectarian war against Iran-backed Shiite militias in central Iraq.

The withdrawal of U.S. troops from Iraq began in December 2007. The last U.S. troops left by December 2011 in accordance to an official agreement between the Iraqi and U.S. governments. As of today there are around 5000 U.S. military personnel deployed in Iraq to advise and assist local forces fighting ISIS militants as well as to support the Iraqi army with training and logistics. The withdrawal of the U.S. troops left a power vacuum and a broken political system which in turn escalated into a sectarian conflict.

Syria

Also in 2011, when the *Arab Spring* revolutions moved to Syria, and Syria's President Bashar al-Assad began bombing and shooting his own people, the Syrian uprising turned into a full-scale civil war. Bashar al-Assad inherited power from his father in July 2000. But since March of 2011, his rule over Syria has been under threat, with the country overrun by violence that has killed an estimated 465,000 people and implicated regional and world powers in the conflict. Despite Western and Arab countries backing the opposition, Assad has survived 7 years of war (with the assistance of Russia, Iran and Lebanese movement Hezbollah) and refuses to step aside. In 2013, Assad came under fire from countries around the world, for using chemical weapons against civilians. By 2017, following news of another round of chemical weapons unleashed on civilians, the United States -in collaboration with great Britain and France- ordered air raids on a Syrian airbase and criticized Russia for supporting his regime.

Al Qaeda renamed itself ISIS (Islamic State in Syria and Iraq) as it saw an opportunity to establish a presence on Syrian ground. It took advantage of the chaos in both Syria and Iraq to expand its control. ISIS fought against the government forces of Syria's President Bashar al-Assad and gained considerable ground throughout the region. Assad and the ruling party in Syria belong to the Alawi sect of Islam, which is closer to the Shiites. The regime is secular in nature, yet it was perceived by ISIS as a threat to the Sunni power in the region and to its ultra-strict interpretation of Islam.

By 2013, ISIS had officially expanded into neighboring Syria. ISIS's rule spread quickly in both countries in an attempt to create an Islamic state ruled by Sharia law (a strict religious code based on traditional interpretation of Islamic practices). In 2014, ISIS took control of the major Iraqi cities of Tikrit, Fallujah and Mosul and declared itself a caliphate or a territory ruled by a caliph (leader).

ISIS became known around the world for its acts of extreme brutality, including public executions, rape, beheading of journalists and crucifixions. Their treatment of Christians in the region was particularly heinous. They earned an atrocious reputation for posting online acts of violence.

Their attacks on humanity weren't limited to people; it also targeted historical sites. They destroyed numerous historical monuments, ancient ruins, museums, churches, temples, mosques, shrines and all kind of priceless treasures throughout Iraq, Syria and Libya, claiming those statues and shrines were against Islamic teachings. Most notably was the destruction of the city of Palmyra (a World Heritage site since 1980), where ISIS committed horrifying acts. The terrorist organization didn't limit its massacres to people but wanted to eradicate any form of culture and civilization.

New reports have indicated that, as of 2017, ISIS has weakened both militarily and financially. The group lost control of large amounts of territory in Iraq. Several of its leaders have been killed or captured. While significant gains against ISIS have been made, international efforts to control this terrorist organization will likely continue for years to come. Various countries—including the United States, Great Britain, France, Russia and several Arab nations— have increased efforts to defeat ISIS. In 2014, a U.S.-led coalition started airstrikes against targets in Iraq and Syria. Today, under the Trump administration, those efforts are consistent and show positive results on the ground. ISIS has been pushed back and denied control of territory as coalition forces are fighting the group in its last strongholds. While the terrorist group is a shadow of its former self, it remains a potent enemy in the territory it once controlled and still has the ability to inspire attacks abroad.

A major issue of contention for the United States is the lack of agreement with Russia over the future of Syria. The U.S. is hesitant about supporting Syria's President Assad and allowing him to stay in power. Despite Russia being on the side of defeating ISIS, the extreme violence shown by President's Assad's Russian-backed regime remains unacceptable by Western and American standards.

What are the effects of ISIS brutality around the world? Terrorism became a common occurrence around the globe. No country was spared attacks, either directly or indirectly funded or inspired by ISIS. To name a few, Iraq, Syria, Turkey, Egypt, Tunisia, Yemen, Lebanon, Indonesia, Pakistan, Afghanistan, Saudi Arabia, Libya, Denmark, Belgium, France, Spain, Great Britain, Germany, Australia, Canada, the United States and more were targets of those terror attacks in different shapes and forms.

Another result of the Iraqi and Syrian civil wars is the refugee crisis. Most notably the Syrian conflict has created one of the worst humanitarian crises of our time. The ruthlessness of the Syrian regime mixed with the utmost brutality of the fighting al-Qaeda factions, such as ISIS and the Al-Nusra Front, eradicated an entire population. Half the country's population (more than 11 million people) have been killed or were forced to flee their homes. Neighboring Lebanon has taken about 1.5 million Syrians (making up 25% of Lebanon's population in a country of four million people). What was originally an act of neighborly generosity and humanitarianism turned into a monumental problem. The refugees became a burden on the Lebanese economy and social structure, creating a political crisis. Government ministries and humanitarian agencies struggle daily to cope with the numbers. Lebanon would like to see the refugees return home, but most of them are afraid of persecution by either the Syrian regime or the fighting factions. The overwhelming majority have no homes to return to.

Other countries in the region (such as Jordan, Turkey, Iraq and Egypt) have also hosted refugees. Today, a total number of approximately five million Syrian refugees are found around the world. Many of them traveled across the Mediterranean to be granted protection in European countries, notably Germany, who took more than half a million refugees. Contrary to popular belief, the United States took only about eight thousand Syrians and granted them asylum on a temporary basis.

This section is an eye-opener as to the results of U.S. policies around the world in general and in the Middle East in particular. Obviously no one could have predicted the amplitude of the monster unleashed after the U.S. invasion and subsequent occupation of Iraq. In its quest to remove a dictator and impose "democratic values" on oil-rich Iraq, the Bush administration failed to grasp the realities on the ground. Iraq was not ready for western values and the U.S. troops on its soil were perceived by many as occupiers. The U.S. presence legitimized the formation of resisting factions which eventually led to massive civil war. Ironically, the primary enemy became the United States and its so-called "self-serving" policies in the region. The Bush administration simply did not foresee the horrific results of its interference in Iraq. It was not supposed to be this way. Removing Saddam Hussein was meant to begin an era of "prosperity", "stability" and "democracy" for Iraq. Instead it reached the exact opposite result. The U.S.

high-risk effort to stabilize an oil-rich nation and impose a new status quo created severe and unforeseeable consequences.

This being said, the anti-Western feeling has always existed in this part of the world, it was simply amplified by the foreign occupation. Our role as a superpower on the global stage is to lead, yet the results are not always positive and policies need to be weighed in carefully before engaging in international conflicts.

Food for Thought

Several questions arise: Can democracy be promoted from outside or imposed by military invasion? Is there a choice between democracy and stability? Most importantly, does leading for the United States mean trying to find solutions or interfering as the policeman of the world?

Each role may have its risks. There is a lesson for future leaders and policy makers as to that role. We were indirectly responsible for the creation of a militant group that is still terrorizing the world with its brutality. We also have a moral responsibility as to the refugee crisis that resulted from our policies. Was it intentional? Certainly not. Could it have been prevented with more thorough and historically responsible policies? I leave that as your food for thought with respect to this section.

In the real world, as lived and experienced by real people, the demand for human rights and dignity, the longing for liberty and justice and opportunity, the hatred of oppression and corruption and cruelty is reality.

—John McCain

X.
THE FAR EAST:
CHINA, JAPAN AND THE KOREAS

This section will focus on the Far East or *East Asia*. Since the mid-19th century, the United States has been a Pacific power and has dominated East Asia. U.S. power and influence was consolidated after WWII and the defeat of Japan. Consequently, this part of the world is vital for U.S. foreign policy. However, for the last few decades, the region has witnessed the rise of a new power, China. This rise is precipitating a power transition. We are therefore observing an adjustment of U.S. policy in the region to counter and contain the rise of China.

The Far East region is one of the fastest growing in the world. It has a wealth of natural resources and low cost labor creating a friendly environment for trade partnerships to flourish. We will discuss the United States relations with four East Asian nations that have affected current U.S. policies: China, Japan, South Korea and North Korea. It is difficult to summarize the complex U.S. relationships with all four nations in such a brief context. I will thus try my best to start with bilateral relations, then focus on geopolitical dynamics.

China

China is a major political and economic power on the global stage. As of 2018, China has the world's second-largest economy only after the United States. Let's begin with a quick overview of some recent history. In 1949 the People's Republic of China was founded when Mao Zedong's Communist Revolution took over the mainland and pushed the Nationalists onto the island of Taiwan.

The United States went to war in Korea and Vietnam, partly to prevent the expansion of Chinese communism -in addition to containing Soviet hegemony-. The U.S. did not formally recognize Communist China for decades after its founding. Instead it recognized the government in Taiwan as the only legitimate representative of the Chinese people.

By 1972, The Nixon administration re-established relations with the People's Republic of China. Both countries were concerned about the rising power of the Soviet Union. In other words, China and the U.S. worked on improving bilateral relations in an attempt to balance growing Soviet influence in the Far East. At this point, it was essential for the United States to develop a new relationship with China in order to preempt a potential Chinese rapprochement with the Soviet Union as well as enlist China's help in this part of the world. The vision was farsighted and laid the cornerstones of U.S.-Chinese future cooperation.

In the late 1970s, Chinese leader Deng Xiaoping sought to bring China closer to Western thinking and to open the economy. This occurred without political liberalization as the regime remained authoritarian in nature. The purpose was to steer away from the Marxist ideology of Mao Tse Tung which had negative effects on China's economic development. The result of this new economic policy was the rise of the Chinese economy. Today China has a population of about 1.4 billion people and an economy to match. The *"bottom-up"* reform movement eventually led to a dynamic market economy sanctioned by the state. Constraints on entrepreneurship and trade were gradually relaxed.

It would be misleading, however, to say that China has turned its back completely on Marxism and state planning. Free-market economy remains limited in nature as there are no widespread private property rights, no independent judiciary to enforce those rights and the government remains very much involved in planning and executing policies. Human rights abuses are prevalent.

In 1989, the Tiananmen Square massacre and the end of the Cold War reshaped U.S.–Chinese relations. As China and the U.S. grew closer economically, their foreign policies diverged. China's lack of respect for human rights, its persistent efforts to steal American technology and its increasingly growing military power became an impediment to future cooperation and trust.

The United States and China have the two largest economies in the world; their bilateral financial and trading relationships shape the global economy. Trading is a priority, but trust is very low, mostly due to diametrically opposed foreign and national security policies. For example, they disagree on how to deal with "rogue" states, such as North Korea, Syria, Zimbabwe, Sudan or Iran. They also fundamentally disagree on human rights. China remains an authoritarian dictatorship under the rule of one party, the Communist Party, with no individual liberties or freedom.

It is important to note that the U.S. trade deficit with China is up to $375 billion as of 2017. The trade deficit exists because U.S. imports from China are as high as $506 billion while exports to China are only $130 billion.

While the U.S. military is still superior, China has narrowed the gap with its anti-satellite systems and anti-ship ballistic missiles to counter the United States' armaments. The Chinese military also constitutes a threat due to hackers who regularly break into U.S. and Western military computers in order to analyze weaknesses. Other Pacific nations (such as Japan, the Philippines, Thailand, South Korea and even Australia) worry about Chinese intentions. Cybersecurity has become a major issue of disagreement between China and the United States as the potential damage is quite large not only affecting the military sphere but also the financial sector.

Recently the Trump administration has attempted a rapprochement with the Chinese leadership. But imposing tariffs on certain Chinese goods eventually led to an escalation when the Chinese government didn't hesitate to retaliate. Today, the United States and China are locked in an ongoing trade war as each country has introduced new tariffs on respective goods. The Trump administration's main goal is to lower the trade deficit with China. In this context, the tariffs are necessary to protect *intellectual property* of U.S businesses and to help reduce the trade deficit. In order to achieve this goal, the administration is attempting to prevent what it deems as "unfair trade practices" that are harming American businesses.

For the longest time, the United States has managed to keep China at bay; it is neither an enemy nor a friend. The U.S. worked with China, when our interests coincided with theirs, and criticized China when conflicts arose. As a foreign policy objective, the United States has sought to build a positive and cooperative relationship with China. Historically, the bilateral relations between the two nations are strong yet complex. They have an extremely extensive trade partnership which necessitates a degree of positive political relations, yet significant issues exist. Managing the U.S.-China relationship is crucial for global stability.

Japan

What about Japan? Japan is one of the world's most effective democracies and economies. Since the end of WWII, and specifically in 1960, the American-Japanese Alliance has been central to U.S. security interests in Asia as well as to regional stability and prosperity.

After the defeat of Japan in WWII, the United States occupied Japan and implemented widespread military, political, economic and social reforms for the purpose of rebuilding the country which was destroyed by the Allied forces and eradicating its past *war-prone* mentality. Today, the United States and Japan not only share the same values but also the same regional strategic interests. Those vital interests and values include the promotion of political and economic freedom throughout the area, the preservation of democratic institutions, support for human rights and, most important, maintaining stability in the Asia-Pacific region. The alliance was strengthened in 2015 with the revised U.S.–Japan Defense Guidelines;

with Japan providing military bases and financial support to U.S. deployed forces, which are essential to maintaining stability in this part of the world.

The United States and Japan cooperate on a broad range of global issues, such as the international diplomatic initiative with regard to dealing with North Korea. The U.S and Japan coordinate regularly with South Korea and Australia when it comes to its North Korea policy.

The U.S. and Japan also have similar goals in the areas of global health, environmental protection (halted by the Trump administration's withdrawal from the Paris Accords on Climate Change), science, technology, space exploration, education, etc.

Japan represents a major market for a wide variety of U.S. goods and services. It exports many products to the United States. Both countries have direct bilateral investments in finance, manufacturing and technology. Today, the Trump administration favors the strengthening of ties and reinforcing of U.S.-Japanese cooperation and friendship.

It is important to note that there has been a mingling of American and Japanese popular culture in the decades following WWII. Japan has exported products to the United States that have deeply influenced American audiences (such as Nintendo, Pokemon, Power Rangers, the Sony PlayStation, and so on) while the United States has infiltrated Japanese society with music, Hollywood movies, celebrities, fashion and sports. The blend has been organic and integral to both societies in turn reinforcing the cultural relationship. The growing number of Japanese coming to the U.S. to visit or live as well as growing Japanese investments in the United States are additional factors prompting interest in Japan. We can safely say that the history of war and hostility between the two nations has not only dissipated, but been replaced by strong mutual respect, shared values, friendly ties and cultural identification.

The Koreas

North Korea (Democratic People's Republic of Korea) remains a difficult and complex problem to solve. The U.S.-North Korea relationship has been historically hostile. After the Korean War, a bloody conflict involving the United States in which three million Koreans died, relations did not normalize. The Korean War, which started on June 25th 1950, was a product of the Cold War between the United States and the Soviet Union. Korea was part of the Japanese empire throughout the first half of the twentieth century. When Japan lost the war, Korea became free and Koreans campaigned for a unified country. However, the United States and the Soviet Union were concerned about their respective spheres of influence in the region. The Soviet Union wanted to spread communist ideology into Korea; the U.S. countered by encouraging the establishment of democracy as well as the forwarding of its policy of *containment*. This disagreement between the two superpowers would eventually lead to the Korean war which was the first battle of the Cold War, and the first major proxy war fought between the United States and the Soviet Union.

As a result of the war, Korea was split into two separate nations along the thirty-eighth parallel. North Korea became a Communist dictatorship backed by the Soviet Union, while South Korea became a U.S.–backed "tentative" democracy. The United States, Japan and their allies helped rebuild South Korea, while North Korea turned to Russia, China and the nations in the Communist sphere of influence for trade and technology.

The United States formally recognizes South Korea (Republic of Korea) as the sole legitimate representative of the Korean people and has, therefore, steadily increased American forces -roughly 29,000- in South Korea in order to defend it against its aggressive northern neighbor. South Korea and the United States agreed to a military alliance in 1953. They called it "the relationship forged in blood". A Combined Forces Command coordinates operations between U.S. units and South Korea's armed forces. In the decades after the war, South Korea experienced political turmoil under autocratic leadership, but developed a vocal civil society that led to protests against authoritarianism. In the 1980s, South korea began the transition to what is now a vibrant democratic system. The United States and South Korea coordinate closely on the denuclearization of the Korean Peninsula. Today, South Korea is a major U.S. ally and trading partner. Their alliance has expanded into a deep comprehensive regional partnership.

South Korea is also a top three origin country for international students attending U.S. colleges and universities.

In recent years, tensions have escalated due to North Korea's testing of nuclear weapons and developing of long-range missiles capable of striking targets thousands of miles away, potentially reaching U.S. soil. Many American presidents have struggled in dealing with this "rogue" state that constitutes a threat to world peace.

For three decades, North Korea's pursuit of nuclear weapons has been the predominant U.S. foreign policy concern on the Korean peninsula. The United States has been both the most important mediator in attempts to resolve the issue diplomatically as well as the leader in global efforts to pressure and isolate North Korea. To this day, those efforts have failed to fundamentally alter the dynamics of conflict on the Peninsula.

American presidents, such as Bill Clinton and George W. Bush, have attempted to reach deals with North Korea, only to see them fall apart. North Korea persisted in its testing of nuclear weapons as the United Nations and the West imposed sanctions. In recent years the testing accelerated to a dangerous level, where experts believe North Korea's weapons can reach the U.S. mainland.

Rhetorics recently escalated between President Trump and Leader Kim Jong-un. The Trump administration took a hard-core approach toward the North Korean regime rejecting any policy of *appeasement.* The situation culminated in a sort of detente as both leaders decided to meet and are today in the process of attempting to reach a denuclearization deal. The unprecedented meeting between a sitting U.S. president and a North Korean leader took place on June 12, 2018, in Singapore. A page has been turned.

Despite the efforts of the Trump administration to move forward, few experts believe North Korea will give up its nuclear arsenal any time soon. North Korea is faced with two options: total denuclearization and prosperity or nuclear weapons and confrontation. The United States will not lift the sanctions unless the prospects of a deal is eminent.

As we can see, the history between the United States and the countries of the Far East is complicated to say the least. Old enemies have become strong allies and trading partners; economic cooperation is mixed with high competition, and hopefully the prospects of peace and denuclearization can be reached in the near future.

Food for Thought

We can ask ourselves several questions such as: What are the repercussions of the high tariffs imposed on Chinese goods? Will they lead to an all-encompassing trade war that could negatively impact our own economy? Or will they increase the power of American *will* on bilateral trade? Could this indirectly affect our progress with North Korea? Japan has taken a neutral approach to the Trump administration's new tariff policies. Will that last? Or will Japan attempt its own reprisals? The prospect of denuclearization in the Korean Peninsula has positively impacted the bilateral relations between the United States and North Korea, as well as provided an important role for South Korea as a mediator. Can North Korean leader Kim Jong-un be trusted? Will negotiations reach the ultimate goal of denuclearization and peace confirming the *"righteousness"* of U.S. policies? Or will the diplomatic efforts end in a deadlock that can further erode the position of the United States as a key player in the region? Most importantly, will a potential failure open the door for China to step in and consolidate its own rising power?

Ignorance, the root and stem of all evil.

—Plato

XI.
AFGHANISTAN, PAKISTAN AND INDIA: FRIENDS OR FOES?

In our quest to understand the role of the United States on the world stage, it is important to take a quick look at Central Asia and the impact of American policies in this part of the world. The geographic position of Central Asia makes the region one of significant consequence, both for security concerns and economic possibilities. The region borders nations that are no stranger to international conflicts and crises; to the north Russia, to the east China, to the south, Iran, Afghanistan, Pakistan and India. Today those nation's internal policies and external behavior are critical to U.S. interests. Central Asia's role in global security continues to grow, hence becoming increasingly valuable as a potential partner to the United States. Economically, Central Asia's geographic position makes the region an important link that bridges East and West. Its abundance of valuable natural resources (petroleum, natural gas, uranium, coal, gold, aluminium and silver) adds to its international weight and opens up a vast window of opportunity for the United States to explore.

Afghanistan

Let's begin with Afghanistan. Afghanistan and the United States have a strong and friendly strategic partnership, Afghanistan being one of the United States' major non-NATO allies today.

Following the Soviet invasion of Afghanistan in 1980, the United States firmly supported diplomatic efforts to achieve Soviet withdrawal. During that period, the U.S. provided financial assistance (about $3 billion) to the Mujahideen (Islamist guerrilla fighters in Afghanistan) in order to confront the Soviet occupation. They were also backed by Saudi Arabia and Pakistan, effectively making the Afghan conflict a Cold War proxy war. Those same Mujahideen eventually kicked out the Soviets from Afghanistan and for the most part became known as the Taliban, one of the most extremist and brutal governments to ever rule a modern-day country under a strict Islamic Law or Sharia. They assumed power in 1996 and held control of most of the country until being overthrown by Americans troops in 2001. The Taliban have been condemned internationally for their harsh enforcement of the Sharia Law, which has resulted in the brutal repression of civilians, particularly women. During their rule, the Taliban committed massacres against Afghan civilians, burned fertile land, engaged in human trafficking and destroyed tens of thousands of homes and cultural monuments.

Following the September 11 attacks—believed to be orchestrated by Saudi terrorist Osama Bin Laden, -residing in Afghanistan under asylum as a guest of the Taliban- the United States launched Operation Enduring Freedom, aimed at removing the Taliban from power and ending the influence of the terrorist group Al Qaeda operating from Afghanistan. The Taliban and Al Qaeda were both the new faces of the old Mujahideen.

The operation was successful as U.S. troops overthrew the Taliban government. It was part of the G.W. Bush administration's *"war on terror"*. At this point, the United States supported the new government of President Hamid Karzai by maintaining a high level of troops to combat remaining Taliban insurgency and by reinforcing the authority of the government.

Today U.S. troops are still stationed in Afghanistan, though diminished in number (14,000 in total).

The United States has also taken a leading role in the reconstruction effort of heavily-destroyed Afghanistan, providing billions of dollars in aid to rebuild the security forces, the infrastructure, the roads, the hospitals, the schools and more. In this context, the U.S. actively tried to establish a secure state with democratic institutions, one that protects the rights of women, strengthens civil society and allows the equal participation of Afghanistan's diverse ethnic groups in the political process.

Afghanistan remains an important partner of the United States in the fight against terrorism. The strong bilateral partnership is guided by Enduring Strategic Partnership Agreement signed in 2012. In order to enhance Afghanistan's capabilities as a partner, and to improve the lives of the Afghan people, the U.S. continues to invest money and resources. The "War on Terror" will eventually cost more than $840 billion in Afghanistan alone.

The two nations are therefore friendly allies, even though serious issues exist. The Obama and Trump administrations have both attempted to withdraw the unpopular presence of U.S. troops (unpopular at home as well as in Afghanistan), only to find themselves faced with the threatening alternative of the Taliban returning to power. There is no limit on how long the U.S. forces would stay in Afghanistan or the number of U.S troops remaining on the ground. By 2015, a new agreement was reached between the two nations under which the American Military, aside from advising, training and assisting the Afghan forces, can now carry out missions against the Taliban insurgents and other militant groups threatening American troops or the Afghan government. Under the Trump Administration, the overall mission remains the same.

American policy, as of now, aims to prevent Afghanistan from becoming a base for terrorist groups that target the United States and its allies, as well as to diminish the possibility of Afghanistan reverting back to civil war, which will destabilize the region. Afghan leadership remains weak, corrupt and erratic, which, in turn, could lead to political vacuum.

The weak governance is a continuous breeding ground for further intimidation by Taliban groups scattered around the country.

Why is Afghanistan a friend and a foe? Because it is our close ally officially, yet its leadership is weak, inconsistent and fragmented. It does not always share the same agenda as that of the United States, and its people aren't always supportive of U.S. presence on their soil.

Pakistan

Pakistan has also assumed an important role in American geopolitical interests in Central Asia, particularly after the September 11, 2001 attacks and the subsequent war on terror. By 2002, The United States named Pakistan a major non-NATO ally which allowed Pakistan to become a leading recipient of U.S. aid. In this context, the United States released billions in assistance to Pakistan. The majority of the aid comes from the Coalition Support Fund which is reimbursement to Pakistan for counter-terrorism operations. Additionally, the goal of the U.S. aid program is to secure a stable Pakistan with a strong economy and a tolerant political system. The focus is on energy, economic growth, health, education, civic institutions and more. The main purpose of the aid program is also to avoid any forms of political radicalization and religious extremism by helping maintain socio-economic stability.

Historically, bilateral relations were not always friendly, particularly when the United States approved sanctions against Pakistan for its nuclear weapons program in the 1970s pertaining to its arms race with neighboring India. The territorial dispute over Kashmir has been the main source of conflict and tensions between Pakistan and India since the British partition of 1947. The nuclear arms race as well as the issue of Kashmir have created major regional instability, aggravated by Pakistan's long history of alternating periods of authoritarian military governments and democracy.

Today the U.S- Pakistan relations are particularly strained as both sides regularly criticize each other's strategy in the war on terror. The United States frequently accuses Pakistan of harboring members of the

Taliban and Al Qaeda, most notably Osama Bin Laden, who was captured and killed in 2011 by American Navy SEALs on Pakistani soil. By providing sanctuary to terrorists, the United States believes that Pakistan's actions are destabilizing neighboring Afghanistan and jeopardizing American troops. For this reason, the Trump administration decided to cut down $300 million in aid to Pakistan in 2018.

Another source of contention between the United States and Afghanistan pertains to the U.S. presence on the Pakistani-Afghan border or what is called the Durand Line. Regular confrontations and daily skirmishes occur between American forces deployed in Afghanistan and Pakistani troops guarding the border, which further damage the U.S.–Pakistan alliance.

Why is Pakistan a friend and a foe? There is a need on both sides to cooperate in order to maintain the stability of the region. The national security interests of both nations usually converge primarily for those geopolitical reasons. Yet trust is at an all-time low. To say they are "troubled" allies is an understatement. The United States strongly believes that Pakistan is still harboring and financing terrorists, while the Pakistani government accuses the United States of conducting regular drone strikes on its soil. Those operations are viewed as a persistent attack on Pakistani sovereignty. The perception of the Trump administration as being Islamophobic and isolationist has further alienated Pakistan from the United States. At the popular level, an already existing wave of anti-Americanism is being further fueled by the Trump administration's policies.

India

On the other hand, the last decade has witnessed a warming up of bilateral relations between the United States and India. The Pakistani government is deeply distrustful of the growing U.S. closeness with India, Pakistan's main regional challenger, viewing the collaboration as undermining Pakistani national security interests.

India emerged in the twenty-first century as increasingly vital to U.S. foreign policy. India is not only a dominant nuclear power in Central Asia but also a dynamic growing nation with a population of 1.3 billion as of 2017. It is perceived as a potential counterweight to the growing influence of China. In other words, balancing China's rise in world affairs, and more specifically in the Indo-Pacific region, is a clear national security interest as well as strategic goal for both the United States and India. This being said, India is often reluctant to get involved in any U.S.-China direct confrontation.

The United States and India have been pursuing a strategic partnership based on shared values and convergent national security interests, particularly when it comes to the "war on terror" and the stability of the Central Asian region. India is perceived by the U.S. a "rising democratic power in a dynamic Asia" and a "major defense partner". The United States and India share similar democracies; broadly pluralistic and vibrant societies based on a multitude of races, ethnicities, cultures, languages and religions. They also share the respect of democratic institutions and the rule of law.

It is important to note that a vast Indian-American community exists in the United States, reflected in the U.S. Congress as well as by the large number of Indian students attending American colleges and universities. The strong people-to-people ties are another source of strength for the partnership. Both countries share significant bilateral trade, investments and billions in sale of oil and military equipment. India's rapidly growing economy has opened the door for American industries to expand abroad, especially in the sectors of technology, manufacturing, engineering and medicine. It is safe to say that U.S.-India relations have never been so wide ranging and multidimensional. As far as India is concerned, the United States remains the ultimate breeding ground for innovation and technology, and the destination for millions of its aspiring youth in the realms of business and education.

Recently several areas of friction arose between the two nations, particularly related to the Trump administration's protectionist measures. Tariffs on steel and aluminum have only added to an increasing list of differences over intellectual property rights and access to certain markets. Also major disagreements arose with regards to India's dependence on Iranian oil under the threat of sanctions from the Trump administration. Another area of dissent pertains to India's reliance on Russian weaponry and the U.S. withdrawal from the Paris Accord on Climate Change.

Despite those frictions, India remains a trusted ally. Why a potential foe? The threat of economic sanctions from the United States is perceived as a flagrant disregard for Indian sovereignty in matters of international relations and an attempt to dictate policy decisions that do not correspond to India's interests.

Food for Thought

To summarize, the Central Asian area of the world is crucial to American interests, yet the bilateral relationships remain extremely blurry. On the one hand, there are formal alliances and common national security interests; on the other hand, a mutual lack of trust and a disregard for policies may escalate into a full-blown animosity, intensified by already-existing tensions. Are we witnessing the continuity of those vital partnerships or are the prevailing anti-american sentiments in the region eroding the foundations of our alliances? How about the India-Pakistan relations? Will they be further aggravated by U.S. policies in the region? Will a potential escalation between those two nations affect the fragile status quo in Afghanistan and impact the security of U.S troops on the ground?

The price of freedom is eternal vigilance.

—Thomas Jefferson

CONCLUSION:
AMERICA'S ROLE IN THE
WORLD TODAY

I would like to end this book with a small insight about the United States' position in the world today, its role as a superpower and its influence on international relations. We started our political enlightenment process with the U.S. Constitution and the internal structure of government, it is thus natural to end it with some thoughts about our relevance on the global stage. What is also important is to understand where we stand *now* after being the major superpower that has led the world since WWI and has influenced all aspects of international affairs.

Exceptionalism

Let's begin with the concept of *"exceptionalism"*. Most Americans, but also others around the world, believe the United States is an *"exceptional"* nation. The term, which stands for "qualitatively different from all other Western countries," was coined in the great work of Alexis de Tocqueville, Democracy in America. Exceptionalism does not only mean "different" and "unique". Many other nations share those characteristics. Exceptionalism requires something far more; a belief that the United States follows a path of history different from the norms that govern other countries. It is not just different, it is an *exception*. It is the bearer of liberty and freedom, and morally superior to others. President Ronald Reagan promoted the image of America as "the shining city upon a hill". In other words, a difference in quality and content.

What makes America unique? After gaining independence from Britain, the first people who populated North America sought a new destiny, based on the recognition of their own values and ideas. They also sought a new national identity. America became the New World, a nation which supports human rights, liberties, wealth, government, life and God, all refined to create a better place than old-world Europe. "Exceptionalism" became part of the national character for the United States.

Today the meaning is closely related to America being a symbol of opportunity, wealth and political weight but also equality and cultural diversity. Throughout its history, the United States has successfully assimilated immigrants. Generation after generation, people have become *"Americanized"*, unlike Europe for example, where the assimilation of immigrants has been a more challenging process. This is due to the fundamental differences between American and European societies and their conception of citizenship. The evidence is clear that the assimilation is real and measurable. Over time, immigrants who arrived to the United States came to resemble natives, and their offsprings formed distinct identities as Americans. In other words, they did not remain foreigners, preserving their old ways of life, but integrated into the dominant American culture even when maintaining some of their traditions. This is not to say that there hasn't been hostility toward immigrants over the years; many in this country have viewed immigrants as a threat to the "integrity" of the nation's culture. But data shows that assimilation has been extremely successful compared to other nations, mostly due to our basic understanding of who we are as Americans as well as the nature of our cultural environment, which for the most part, welcomes diversity as part of the national identity. The *American Dream*, or the perception that Americans enjoy high social mobility, plays a key role in attracting immigrants from all over the world, mostly those who just like Americans, are characterized and driven by a strong work ethic, competitiveness and individualism.

One can also argue that America's exceptionalism stems from its unique position on the world stage as the only power superior to "all others in all matters". A civilization that is also *morally* superior destined to guide the world. Indeed, the United States is one of the richest and one of the most economically, militarily and technologically advanced nations in history. Its gross domestic product (GDP) accounts for close to the quarter of the world's total, and its military budget is almost as much as the world's defence spending put together. It is the only *true* global power. Its military reach extends to every point on the globe and most international institutions reflect American interests.

The U.S. has been a leader in technological innovation and scientific research since the end of the 19th century. By the 20th century, it has also become a major source of international cultural influence and appeal reflected in Hollywood movies, American TV, jazz, blues, rock and roll, rap music, the fashion industry and much more.

Countries around the globe look for American leadership, help and guidance. They also take into account U.S. reaction and retaliation. The United States' dominant global position, politically, economically, and militarily allows it to pressure allies, impose economic sanctions as well as inflict military reprisals. In this context, the U.S. has been labeled a "*bully*" with regards to imposing its will on other nations and dictating outcomes in world affairs. Today, American exceptionalism is increasingly linked to military hegemony.

It is important to note that the United States has never been a traditional imperial power -such as Great Britain, France and the Ottoman Empire or in the more distant past Rome and Greece-. It is unique among past hegemonic nations in not seeking to expand its power through *territorial gains*. Its leadership position prompts other nations to seek its assistance in addressing their problems, and at the same time, to resent it for "meddling" in their internal affairs. It is an ambivalent global role inherited from its unique position as a superpower but not an imperial or colonial nation. To a great extent, this uniqueness reflects the exceptionalism of America and the American national character; being more powerful militarily than any nation on earth, it could have sought territorial expansion. But the United States follows a path of history that is different from any other nation past or present, and is not governed by the same set of norms that have propelled previous hegemonic powers to expand all over the world.

Exceptionalism can also be linked to other values, such as spreading democracy and attempting to establish it as an ideology in other nations. After WWII, the United States witnessed the pinnacle of its global influence in what is recognized as Pax Americana. The U.S. managed global order by maintaining relative peace and security in the Western Hemisphere. It started with the launching of the Marshall Plan in 1948 which contributed over $15 billion to rebuild Western Europe and to prevent the spread of communism. From this point forward, U.S. foreign policy goals included promoting world peace and security as well as maintaining a balance of power among other major powers. Creating an international order in which more people are free and prosperous was perceived to be profoundly in America's best interest. After the Cold War ended, promoting the international spread of democracy replaced the policy of containment. The idea of democratization seems to become America's mission for many reasons, including the best interest of the citizens of the new "tentative" democracies, economic development -creating new trade partners-, the promotion of world peace, and of course the serving of U.S. national interests. Democracies rarely, if ever, go to war among each other. Therefore, democratization can only promote the prospects of lasting international peace.

This leads us to the question of whether America has become a non-traditional *imperial power* in its quest to spread its values around the globe. In this context, the connotation has a negative effect, since often we have seen a failure -as well as resistance- on the part of developing countries to adopt those American values that are alien to their own identities and perceived as imposed by an assertive foreign power. Afghanistan, Iraq, Libya, and Yemen are visible examples of failure. Military invasions, followed by occupation and rebuilding, have not always reached the best results, even when the intentions were to implement democratic values and basic human rights. The United States seems genuinely convinced that liberal democratization is the only viable political formula and made the promotion of democracy a key element of U.S foreign policy. The goal itself is arguably the best solution for replacing autocracies and spreading peace. The question is, however, how can those goals be implemented without the internal conflicts and violence that have resulted upon attempting to do so? There are many dangers associated with democratic *transitions*. Direct military interventions for the purpose of imposing democracy have backfired. One can not create democratic institutions in countries that have no effective legal systems, no understanding of pluralism, no decent level of education or income, combined with a high level of corruption and most importantly deep-rooted religious and tribal affiliations. Using force to spread democracy almost always triggers violent resistance as most people do not appreciate following orders from a foreign occupier. To believe the U.S. military could simply *export* democracy remains an overconfident and non realistic perception of the developing world, and a primary reason behind the labeling of the United States by many as a nontraditional *imperial* power.

Yet, to this day, the United States remains the nation with the highest level of global leadership and activism in international affairs, aspiring to promote international law and human rights when possible. In this context, The United States actively pursues the goal of a peaceful, prosperous, democratic and equitable world. There is a deep-rooted belief that the only way to build a stable global economy is to make sure other nations are also secure and are developing in the right direction. Hence the enormous amounts of foreign aid the U.S. allocates to other countries on a regular basis. According to the World Economic Forum, the United States ranks first in the world when it comes to foreign aid, followed by Germany, Great Britain, France and Japan. In 2015, it gave over $30 billion either as direct bilateral aid or through international organizations such as the UN and the World Bank. As humanitarian crises continue around the world, foreign aid remains extremely important in order to counter those crises and stimulate economic growth. In this context, the United States has achieved incredible results while helping people around the world fight poverty, hunger, health crisis and dictatorship. Both the direct or indirect assistance has had a huge positive impact internationally and relieved numerous humanitarian crises. With its generosity throughout the decades, the United States has indeed shown its exceptional character.

Obviously a double standard exists. As I mentioned above, our foreign policy has often been self-serving and has led to conflicts around the world. Some backfired into chaos. Fighting for ideology and influence—such as the case in Korea and Vietnam—led to bloody turmoil and enmity. Removing dictators—such as the case in Afghanistan, Iraq and Libya—ended up being a military and economic long-term burden, combined with civil wars and in some cases the spread of terrorism. Foreign military interventions have not always led to the best results, even with the best of intentions.

In the past, the United States has often dictated solutions from afar without determining whether they could be realistically implemented on the ground. Since the military drawbacks in Iraq and Afghanistan, U.S. policies -particularly under the Obama administration- shifted slowly toward a different approach, one of respecting the unique partnerships with other nations instead of imposing self-serving agenda. Partnerships built on consultation rather than command are more likely to achieve long lasting results.

The most effective tool historically, has been *diplomacy*. When there is a true committed movement in favor of democracy from *within* -as in the case of Eastern Europe at the end of the Cold War or Myanmar more recently- powerful nations such as the United States can use more subtle forms of persuasion to encourage gradual transitions. We have done this successfully on a number of occasions, for example in South Korea or the Philippines. Non military tools such as diplomacy and sanctions have proven to be more effective long-term solutions. In these cases, the pro-democracy movements have been building for many years and enjoyed broad grassroot support by the time they gained power, contrary to societies -such as in the Middle East region- were pluralism is still a foreign concept. Diplomacy may not have the fast results of quickly removing dictators as military invasions, but it has proven to be more successful foreign policy tool in the long term.

Contributing to economic development is also critical to the success of our defense missions abroad, particularly where weak governments, turmoil and poverty encourage instability. New technologies and innovations are allowing struggling nations to step into the 21st century and to overcome various obstacles. In other words, achieving true progress may have proven to be difficult, but not impossible.

Is America first and foremost? Should it be first and foremost?

Globalism versus Isolationism

Today, and after the election of President Donald Trump in 2016, many have re-evaluated the role of the United States in the world. The question pertaining to isolationism versus globalism has become more relevant in international affairs. Should America pursue its globalist trend started after WWII? Globalism, up to this point, has been seemingly unstoppable. By globalism, we mean the leading role of America in the world, its interaction with other countries through trade agreements, military alliances, environmental policies, foreign aid, financial linkages—in brief, increased economic integration and partnership with the rest of world.

Without globalization, America would not have defeated communism. For much of the 20th century, geopolitics drove American foreign policy. The United States strived to prevent any single country from dominating the centers of strategic power in Europe and other areas of the world. To that end the United States fought two world wars and the Cold War. The collapse of the Soviet Union ended the last serious challenge for territorial dominance. The most important goal of U.S. foreign policy was achieved. The 1990's witnessed the consolidation of that success. Together with its European allies, the United States created, for the first time in history, a peaceful, undivided and democratic Europe; Pax Americana at its best.

It is safe to say that globalization is in a way an American invention because no one has shaped world trade, technology and military influence more than the spread of globalism under the leadership of the United States. The success of American policy over the past few decades meant that no power -not Russia nor Germany nor a United Europe nor Japan nor even China- poses a hegemonic threat to American interests and influence in the world.

Globalization has also encouraged the spread of ideas and information across the Internet and prompted people in different regions of the world to challenge autocratic rulers and advance the cause of basic human rights and democracy. Without cooperation some crucial problems would become extremely difficult to solve unilaterally. Climate change is probably the most obvious case, but others include stopping the spread of weapons of mass destruction and fighting international terrorism.

The trend seems to be shifting today. A new wave of America first and foremost is rising. Do we really need our allies, such as NATO members? Do we really need our trading partners, such as Canada and Mexico? Should we accept the Chinese products cheaply invading our markets instead of imposing higher tariffs? Why is India appropriating our intellectual properties? Can Saudi Arabia still impose high oil prices? Should we be subject to international cooperation and "unfavorable" bilateral agreements? Why should we incur the heaviest cost in defending Europe? Will NATO remain our sole responsibility? And so on. Much of the foreign policy debate in the United States today revolves around rethinking the fundamental importance of globalization versus *American primacy*. Shouldn't the United States use its predominant position to gets its way, *regardless* of what others want? Isn't America first and foremost?

Isolationism isn't a foreign concept in our history -it actually originated with the Founding Fathers themselves-. Before WWI the policy of non-involvement or non-interventionism was the norm. This school of thought advocates that governments should not prioritize foreign affairs. In fact, nations should avoid any forms of alliances with other nations in order to avoid being drawn into wars. Neutrality should be the primary drive of our foreign policy, as we are not responsible for other nations entanglements, therefore not accountable for their behavior. Isolationism also extends to the economic sphere, it advocates the rejection of restrictive trade agreements and encourages protectionist measures for our products. Instead the focus should be solely on domestic issues and policies. By turning our back on the problems of the world, we can focus more intently on our own affairs, particularly decreasing investments in foreign aid, eliminating military interventions abroad and lessening trading ties; which in turn will allow us to improve the circumstances for citizens domestically.

By not getting involved in international conflicts, the need to maintain an expensive military decreases. The savings could in turn be spent on domestic programs that would benefit the citizens and develop the country. Are we moving toward this trend? Certainly the Trump administration is attempting to reshape, renegotiate or even end trading agreements with several of our allies and partners. The Trump administration is seeking to increase tariffs on foreign products, targeting international friends as well as foes. Yet to imply that the Trump administration is isolationist in nature remains far from reality. Today, the United States is still very much involved in international negotiations, conflict resolutions as well as military ventures. The U.S. is not pursuing an isolationist policy regardless of certain similarities. Notwithstanding an ever-growing sense of *nationalism*, there is a much deeper issue to deal with: economics which is unavoidably global, has surpassed politics, which is mostly domestic. In other words, it is impossible in the modern era to return to purely isolationist policies despite the politics of nationalism. The trend is irreversible.

While military spending is still on the rise -U.S. military budget now exceeds $700 billion-, the Trump administration is questioning the validity of NATO and taking a hard position vis-à-vis our military allies. The trend seems to be shifting *inward*, as the Trump administration is pursuing its *America-first* policy and slowly relinquishing its vanguard role in the world as the leader and promoter of international relations. Some have labeled the Trump policies as *neo-isolationist*. Those policies promote America's interests above and beyond all others, including our allies, yet are still very much engaged in upholding -if not increasing- the United State's global hegemonic status. Today, U.S. military activism has not diminished the least bit.

Will this new trend benefit America? Is it *sustainable*? When trade agreements with other nations are put aside due to *protectionist* policies, it can potentially affect the strength of the economy at home. Some might say a strong and dynamic economy can only exist with solid and binding trade agreements between nations. Others argue the opposite. They believe that focusing on domestic policies and applying protectionist measures promote peace as well as wealth internally. Yet, it is unrealistic to characterize the Trump administration's policies as isolationist. Despite anti-immigration rhetorics and a nationalist agenda, the administration's foreign policy is ambitious and globally involved. The long-term vision might be isolationist as far as promoting America's interests above all others and encouraging national sovereignty, but the reality of American diplomatic, economic and military presence all over the world is still very much alive. Traditional isolationism implies disengagement, if not total retreat, from world affairs. It is certainly not the case today.

I will leave it up to you, the reader, to weigh in on what trends will strengthen and fortify our country in the near future and for decades to come.

Today we are witnessing the slowing down of democratic ideals globally. With the new waves of conflicts and immigration, various nations are forced to pick between those democratic ideals and their own national identity. Many are choosing identity, including the United States. Once a leader in promoting and spreading the values of our Constitution—liberty, democracy, individualism, unity, integration and diversity—today the United States is turning inward toward the quest for identity. It is seeking new allies and criticizing old friends. There seems to be an erosion in the long-standing pillars of American diplomacy: effectiveness, reliability and the image of a dependable strong ally committed to solving the world's most difficult problems.

Food for Thought

The questions remain: Are we witnessing the end of Pax Americana? Is the U.S. breaking decades of alliances, forcing our allies to seek their own path? The United States has fought two world wars and a Cold war to achieve peace and stability in the Western hemisphere. Are we slowly relinquishing our leadership role in world affairs? Are we paving the way for China and others to step in? Or are we simply redefining a *new era* on the global stage? The answers are yet to come.

BIBLIOGRAPHY

Ahmad, Javid. "Mistrust Is the Original Sin of US–Pakistan Relations." The Hill, 8 January 2018.

Ahmed, Nafeez. "Iraq Invasion was about Oil." The Guardian, 20 March 2014.

Amadeo, Kimberly. "US Trade Deficit with China and Why It's So High." The Balance, 5 October 2018.

Al Jazeera. "Profile: Bashar al-Assad. President Assad has ruled Syria with an iron fist for nearly two decades. We take a look at his life and legacy." Al Jazeera Media Network, 17 April 2018.

Al Jazeera. "UN: Number of Syrian Refugees Passes Five Million." Al Jazeera Media Network at Aljazeera.com, 30 March 2017.

Bajoria, Jayshree, and Youkyung Lee. "The US–South Korea Alliance." Council on Foreign Relations, 13 October 2011.

Bard, Mitchell. "U.S.-Israel Relations: American Public Opinion Toward Israel." Jewish Virtual Library, March 2018.

Barnard, Anne. "For Syrian Refugees, There Is No Going Home." The New York Times, 23 February 2017.

Bennett, Andrew, and Ikenberry, John G. "The Review's Evolving Relevance for U.S Foreign Policy 1906-2006." American Political Science Review, 2006.

Bickerton, Ian J, Klausner, Carla L. A History of the Arab-Israeli Conflict. New York: Pearson Higher Education, 2009.

Bowlby, Chris. "Germany: Reluctant Military Giant?" BBC Radio 4 Analysis, 12 June 2017.

Bremmer, Ian. "ISIS Is a Multinational Organization Drawing Fighters from Around the World." @IANBREMMER, 14 April 2017.

Byman, Daniel L. "Iraq and the Global War on Terrorism." Brookings Press, 1 July 2007.

Cameron, Maxwell A. The Making Of NAFTA: How the Deal Was Done. New York: Cornell University Press, 2002.

Camp, Roderic A. Mexico: What Everyone Needs to Know. New York: Oxford University, 2011.

Cárdenas, José R. "The US–Mexico Relationship Has Survived and Thrived under Trump." FP, Elephants in the Room blog post, 22 March 2018.

Castle, Stephen, and De Freytas-Tamura, Kimiko. "Trump Visit Tests Britain's 'Special Relationship' with U.S." The New York Times, 11 July 2018.

Cecco, Leyland. "Prepare for the Worst: souring Canada-US relations fuel worries of trade war." The Guardian, 11 June 2018.

Chanlett-Avery, Emma, and Rinehart, Ian E. "The US–Japan Alliance." Washington, DC: Congressional Research Service, 9 February 2016.

Charillon, Frédéric. "The Ups and Downs of Franco-American Relations." The Conversation, 19 July 2017.

Cheng, Dean. "The Complicated History of US Relations with China." The Heritage Foundation, 11 October 2012.

Clinton, Hillary, and FP Staff. "Development in the 21st Century." Center for Global Development in Washington, D.C. , 6 January, 2010.

Cohen, Andrew. "Canadians: More than Not Americans." Policy Options Politiques, 1 March 2011.

Cohen, Josh. "Turning the Tide of U.S.-Russia Relations (Op-ed)." The Moscow Times, 16 August 2018.

Connor, Phillip. "Most Displaced Syrians Are in the Middle East and about a Million Are in Europe." Pew Research Center, 29 January 2018.

Cordesman, Anthony H. "U.S Military Spending: The Cost of Wars." Center for Strategic and International Studies, 10 July 2017.

Daalder, Ivo H, and Lindsay, James M. "The Globalization of Politics: American Foreign Policy for a New Century." Brookings, 1 January 2003.

Davis, Bob, and Lingling, Wei. "US, China Plot Road Map to Resolve Trade Dispute by November." The Wall Street Journal, 17 August 2018.

Davis, James E, and Fernlund, Phyllis and Woll, Peter. Civics: Government and Economics in Action. New Jersey: Prentice Hall, 2009 Edition.

Dehghan, Saeed Kamali. "Nearly half of US arms exports go to the Middle East." The Guardian, 11 March 2018.

De Tocqueville, Alexis. Democracy in America. London: Saunders and Otley, 1835.

DeYoung, Karen. "Putin Speech Adds to Freeze in US–Russia Relations." The Washington Post, 1 March 2018.

Dorn, James A. "The Genesis and Evolution of China's Economic Liberalization." Cato Institute, 22 August 2016.

Erikson, Amanda. "The Long History of Incredibly Fraught Relations between the US and Pakistan." The Washington Post, 5 January 2018.

Erikson, Amanda. "What's Behind the Feud between Saudi Arabia and Iran? Power." The Washington Post, 20 December 2017.

Federman, Josef. "As Gaza Strip deteriorates, Israel turns to world for help." The Times Of Israel, 15 February 2018.

Fergusson, Ian F, and Villarreal, Angelis M. NAFTA at 20: Overview and Trade Effects. Washington, DC: Congressional Research Service, 2014.

Fernandez, Erwin S. "The United States and the Arab-Israeli Conflict: (Un)forging Future Peace." International Social Science Review, Vol. 80, No. 1/2 (2005), 41–50.

Ganesh, Janan. "Isolationism is the wrong charge to level at Donald Trump." Financial Times, 8 August 2018.

Goldenberg, Suzanne. "Chaos and humiliation as Israel pulls out of Lebanon." The Guardian, 23 May 2000.

Griffiths, John C. Afghanistan: A History of Conflict. London: Carlton Books, 2001.

Griffiths, James. "Who Are the Key Players in Afghanistan?" CNN, 19 September 2017.

Guzansky, Yoel. "Saudi Foreign Policy: Change of Direction Required." INSS Insight No. 975, 26 September 2017.

Haass, Richard. A World in Disarray: American Foreign Policy and the Crisis of the Old Order. New York: Penguin Books, 2018.

Halaoua, Yona. "Iran, trade, climate: What's at stake on Macron's visit to Washington." France 24, 23 April 2018.

Hargrove, Erwin C. "On Canadian and American Political Culture." The Canadian Journal of Economic and Political Science, Vol. 33, No. 1 (Feb. 1967), 107–111.

Hashemi, Nader, and Postel, Danny. "Iran, Saudi Arabia and Modern Hatreds." The New York Times, 15 May 2018.

Hastedt, Glenn, and Lybecker, Donna L, and Shannon, Vaughn P. Cases in International Relations: Pathways to Conflict and Cooperation. California: CQ Press, 2014.

Hoskin, Peter. "How Japan became a pop culture superpower." The Spectator, 31 January 2015.

Iokibe, Makoto, and Tosh, Minohara. The History of US–Japan Relations: From Perry to the Present. Singapore: Palgrave Macmillan, 2017.

Jezard, Adam. "The US and North Korea: a Brief History." World Economic Forum, 19 December 2017.

Kaplan, Laurence S. The United States and NATO: the Formative Years. Kentucky: University Press of Kentucky, 2014.

Kelley, Ninette. "Lebanon, Overrun by Syrian Refugees." The New York Times, 19 June 2013.

Kennedy, Paul. The Rise and Fall of the Great Powers. New York: Random House, 1987.

Kugelman, Michael. "The U.S.-Pakistan Relationship is on Life Support." The National Interest, 4 September 2017.